Beginning Radio and TV Newswriting

BEGINNING RADIO AND TV NEWSWRITING

FIFTH EDITION

A SELF-INSTRUCTIONAL LEARNING EXPERIENCE

K. TIM WULFEMEYER

WILEY-BLACKWELL

A John Wiley & Sons, Ltd., Publication

This fifth edition first published 2009
© 2009 K. Tim Wulfemeyer

Edition history: Iowa State University Press (1e 1976; 2e 1984; 3e 1993; 4e 2003)

Blackwell Publishing was acquired by John Wiley & Sons in February 2007. Blackwell's publishing program has been merged with Wiley's global Scientific, Technical, and Medical business to form Wiley-Blackwell.

Registered Office
John Wiley & Sons Ltd, The Atrium, Southern Gate, Chichester, West Sussex, PO19 8SQ, United Kingdom

Editorial Offices
350 Main Street, Malden, MA 02148-5020, USA
9600 Garsington Road, Oxford, OX4 2DQ, UK
The Atrium, Southern Gate, Chichester, West Sussex, PO19 8SQ, UK

For details of our global editorial offices, for customer services, and for information about how to apply for permission to reuse the copyright material in this book please see our website at www.wiley.com/wiley-blackwell.

The right of K. Tim Wulfemeyer to be identified as the author of this work has been asserted in accordance with the Copyright, Designs and Patents Act 1988.

All rights reserved. No part of this publication may be reproduced, stored in a retrieval system, or transmitted, in any form or by any means, electronic, mechanical, photocopying, recording or otherwise, except as permitted by the UK Copyright, Designs and Patents Act 1988, without the prior permission of the publisher.

Wiley also publishes its books in a variety of electronic formats. Some content that appears in print may not be available in electronic books.

Designations used by companies to distinguish their products are often claimed as trademarks. All brand names and product names used in this book are trade names, service marks, trademarks or registered trademarks of their respective owners. The publisher is not associated with any product or vendor mentioned in this book. This publication is designed to provide accurate and authoritative information in regard to the subject matter covered. It is sold on the understanding that the publisher is not engaged in rendering professional services. If professional advice or other expert assistance is required, the services of a competent professional should be sought.

Library of Congress Cataloging-in-Publication Data

Wulfemeyer, K. Tim.
   Beginning radio-TV newswriting : a self-instructional learning experience/K. Tim Wulfemeyer.—5th ed.
      p. cm.
   Rev. ed. of: Beginning radio-TV newswriting. 4th ed. 2003.
   Includes bibliographical references and index.
   ISBN 978-1-4051-6042-1 (pbk. :alk. paper)
   1. Broadcast journalism—Authorship. 2. Report writing. I. Wulfemeyer, K. Tim. Beginning radio-television newswriting.
II. Title. III. Beginning radio and television newswriting.
   PN4748.B75W8 2009
   808′.06607—dc22

                                          2009001777

A catalogue record for this book is available from the British Library.

Set in 10.5 on 13 pt Minion by SNP Best-set Typesetter Ltd., Hong Kong

01   2009

Contents

PART 3: WRITING INTRODUCTIONS 84

PART 4: ADDING VISUALS 108

Preface

This book will introduce you to some of the basic styles, principles and techniques of radio-TV newswriting. To complete most of the exercises, all you'll need is a pencil or pen and some blank sheets of paper. An audio recorder would be helpful in this learning experience, but it's not necessary.

Follow the instructions in the book carefully. You won't be reading through it page by page; you'll be skipping pages and perhaps even rereading pages. Pay close attention to all directions, but especially those at the bottom of pages.

Learning Objectives: Take a look at the following list of skills you'll have learned when you've finished this book. Using correct radio-TV news style, you'll be able to:

1. Write radio and television news "reader" stories.
2. Write introductions to recorded comments from news makers.
3. Write introductions for reporter packages.
4. Write copy to match pictures and graphics.
5. Write copy to match video.
6. Place attribution in its proper place in a sentence.
7. Place a person's title in its proper place in a sentence.
8. Place a person's age in its proper place in a sentence.
9. Place a person's address in its proper place in a sentence.
10. Place time elements in their proper place in a sentence.
11. Include direct and indirect quotations in copy.
12. Include numbers in copy.
13. Include individually voiced numbers and letters in copy.
14. Use active-voice verbs to improve the flow of copy.
15. Use contractions to "informalize" copy.
16. Use the appropriate tense of verbs to increase the immediacy of copy.
17. Use punctuation to increase the clarity of copy.
18. Edit printed copy.

You also will be familiar with some of the terminology used in radio and television news. In addition, you'll be acquainted with some of the basic scripting styles used in radio and television news.

Finally, I'd like to thank my wife, Lori Lynn McFadden Wulfemeyer, who assisted in the writing and editing of this book. Lori is Assistant Dean for Administration at the Thomas Jefferson School of Law. She has taught at San Diego State University and the University of Hawaii and has worked for radio stations in Iowa, California, and Hawaii.

Introduction

In radio-TV newswriting, you're writing for the ear and the eye, not just for the eye as in newspaper writing. A newscaster has to be able to read your copy easily, so you have to make it easy on the eye. And it has to *sound* good to audience members, so you have to make it easy on the ear, too.

Writing for both the ear and the eye is a tricky business. It takes skill and practice to explain complicated issues and events in understandable, simple words, but that's what radio-TV newswriters must do.

Most stories must be told in 15 to 30 seconds. Some very important or complicated stories run a little longer, but rarely does any one story run longer than one minute on the average radio newscast or two minutes on the average television newscast. It's not easy to write a clear, understandable story in simple, direct language that gives the important elements of an event or issue in less than two minutes, and it's especially difficult to accomplish the task in less than 30 seconds.

The most successful radio-TV newswriters write the way people talk in their everyday conversations. Conversational writing is the key. It's the secret of good radio-TV newswriting. Just remember, when you're writing a radio-TV news story, THINK the way you talk and WRITE the way you talk.

Try to write the story the same way you'd tell it to a friend. Think of the entire audience as just one of your friends and write the story as you'd tell it to him or her personally. If you can do that, you're on the way to becoming a professional radio-TV newswriter.

This book will give you some tricks of the trade, guidelines, hints and suggestions that will help you become a successful radio-TV newswriter.

Radio-TV News Terminology

Here are some common terms used in radio-TV news. Look them over BEFORE moving on to Part 1. You'll get more out of this learning experience if you're familiar with some of the jargon used in radio-TV news.

Actuality: Recorded comments from a news source. Used in radio. Also called *tape cut, cut, soundbite* or *bite*.

Actuality Story: Radio news story that contains an *actuality. Newscaster* reads *copy* associated with the *actuality*. Sometimes called a *reader-act*, which is short for *reader* and *actuality*.

Ad-lib: Unscripted comment by a news *anchor* or reporter.

Ambient Noise: The actual, *natural sound*s occurring at the locations where news is being gathered.

Ambient Sound: See *Ambient Noise*.

Anchor: Person who reads news on air. Also called a *newscaster, on-air person, on-air personality* or *talent*.

AP: Short for *associate producer*. Also short for "Associated Press."

Assignment Editor: Person who decides which stories will be covered and which reporters will cover them.

Associate Producer: Person who assists the *producer* of a newscast. Writes, helps organize the newscast, coordinates *character generator* and *teleprompter* efforts.

Audio Tape: Magnetic *tape* used to record sound.

Backgrounding: Doing research on a source or topic/subject prior to conducting an interview or going into the field to gather information.

Background Sound: Actual noises recorded at the scene of a news event or news-gathering activity. *Ambient sound*. Aired at a lower volume than the voice of a reporter or *anchor*. Also called *natural sound, nat sound* or *wild sound*.

Backtiming: Timing a newscast, newscast segment or story from the end to the beginning. Technique used to ensure that no matter what happens during a newscast, a pre-selected segment (story or stories plus *credits* and/or close) will air correctly. Backtiming normally is used to ensure that a newscast ends on time or that a portion of the newscast ends with specific stories or *features*. Example: A *producer* "backtimes" the final segment and determines it's 1:00 long. That means a newscaster must begin the final segment with exactly 1:00 remaining in the newscast. Despite careful planning, newscasters quite often must either read extra stories or cut material in order to begin the final segment at the precise time.

Bars and Tone: Video of colored strips (bars) and a consistent audio sound (tone) used to adjust visual and audio levels of cameras and other technical equipment. Bars and tone often are edited onto the beginning of stories and also used to calibrate studio cameras and microphones.

Bite: Short for *soundbite*. Recorded comments from a news source.

Breaker: Unexpected news event. Examples: fires, traffic accidents, plane crashes, hostage situations, acts of terrorism, murders, tornadoes, floods, earthquakes, hurricanes, avalanches.

Breaking News: See *Breaker*. Also refers to events and issues that occur during a newscast or that occur right before a newscast begins.

Bridge: Transition between story elements, stories or newscast segments. Within a story, a reporter *stand-up* is often used as a bridge.

Briefs: Short news stories—usually about :10–:15 each.

B-roll: Term left over from days when film was used in TV news. Refers to action and activities captured on video. Most often used in connection with providing video to accompany *voice-overs*, reporter *voice tracks* and *soundbites*.

Bulletin: A *breaking news* story of great importance that moves on a wire service. Can also refer to an interruption of regularly scheduled programming by a newscaster to provide information about a *breaking news* story.

Bump: Brief sentence or sentence fragment read by a newscaster or off-screen announcer about an upcoming story or segment. Usually aired before a commercial break. Object is to entice audience members to stay tuned. Titillating aspects of a story often played up. Sometimes called a *bumper, tease, toss* or *promo*.

Bumper: See *Bump*.

Call Letters: The consonants and vowels used to identify a radio or television station. Examples: KTIM, KCTI, WOWA, WETV.

Cart: Short for "cartridge." Plastic shell that contains *audio tape*. Used by some radio stations for actualities, *voicers* and *wraparounds*.

CG: Short for *character generator*.

Character Generator: Computer-based system used to superimpose letters, numbers and words on a television screen.

Chromakey: Electronic process used to insert *graphics* and other *visual* material behind a television newscaster, sportscaster or weathercaster. A computer *graphic*, picture, *still frame*, video or other *visual* material is electronically substituted for a color, usually blue or green, that is painted on the news *set*.

Chyron (chiron): Brand of *character generator*.

Close-up Shot: Video scene with a restricted field of view. Examples include a hand that fills the TV screen or a single face. Camera usually as close to action as possible or zoomed-in as far as possible.

Copy: News story written to be aired. Can also refer to material that is used to produce a news story (i.e., *source copy* or *wire copy*).

Cover Shot: Video scene that covers a large or wide area. Usually shows much action, lots of people or a large expanse of territory. Also known as an *establishing shot, long shot* or *wide shot*. It establishes the visual parameters for a succeeding series of scenes. Camera usually 15–20 feet from action.

Credits: Superimposed list of names that is seen at the end of TV newscasts. Names include people responsible for putting the newscast on the air and station management personnel.

Crosstalk: Newscaster asks questions of or chats with a reporter after the reporter finishes a live report. Also called a *Q & A* or *De-brief*.

CU: Short for close-up. See *Close-up Shot*.

Cut: Short for *tape cut*. An *actuality* or *soundbite*. Can also refer to the video-editing process or a scene in a video (i.e., "to cut the video" or a "video cut").

Cutaway: A video scene related to the main action, but not a critical part of the action. Used to provide transitions between main scenes and to avoid *jump cuts*.

Dateline: Geographic location where a news story was written and/or placed on a wire service feed. Usually found at the beginning of wire service stories. See *Wire Copy*.

De-brief: See *Crosstalk*.

Developing Story: A type of *breaking news* story. Usually not as immediate or important as a *breaking news* story, but one that is expected to have new developments reasonably soon.

DC: Short for *digital correspondent*.

Digital: A recording, system or piece of equipment in which the output varies in discrete on and off pulses—zeros and ones. Translation of original sound and picture into binary computer language.

Digital Correspondent: Individual reporter who uses *digital* technology and *non-linear editing* to create a finished, ready-to-air story. The reporter acquires all the information, writes the script, creates the *voice track*, plus shoots and edits the video for the story. Also called a *DC, video journalist, VJ* or *one-man band*.

Digital Tape: Like traditional *audio tape* or *videotape*, except audio and video recorded as *digital* signals so they can be edited in and played by a computer.

Donut: Live story that features a reporter *stand-up open*, pre-recorded video and *soundbite*s and then a reporter *stand-up close*.

Drive Time: Weekday hours during which radio listening normally is at its highest because most people are driving to or from work. In most markets, morning drive time runs 6 a.m.–10 a.m. and afternoon drive time runs 3 p.m.–7 p.m.

ENG: Short for "electronic news gathering." Refers to the use of portable *videotape* or *digital* equipment, computers, satellites and other sophisticated technologies.

Enterprise Story: A unique story that has been developed in-house through the use of special sources. It's unlikely that other news organizations would have a similar story. Much like an *exclusive*.

Establishing Shot: See *Cover Shot*.

Evergreen: A story that can be aired just about any time. Little or no time-sensitive content. Usually a *feature* story.

Exclusive: A unique story or piece of information that one station has and others do not.

Executive Producer: Person responsible for overseeing the work of all the newscast *producer*s at a station. Might have primary responsibility for a station's main evening newscast. Also can be in charge of special news programming.

Eyewash Video: Video scenes that are not directly related to what is being read by a newscaster. For example, in a story about test scores for high school students, video of students wandering around campus might be shown. Also called *wallpaper video*.

Fade to Black: At the end of a story, instead of immediately going to the next visual source, a director gradually transitions from a video source to a black screen. Often done with death stories, or highly emotional, issue-oriented stories.

Feature: A "soft" or "light" news story. Examples: *personality profile*s, restaurant reviews, movie reviews, humorous *pieces*. Sometimes called a *people story*. Can be used to describe special newscast segments. Examples: "Keeping Fit," "Troubleshooter" and "Consumer Watch." Can refer to a more serious type of "feature" report. Examples: a feature on safety at the university or a feature on a new cure for baldness.

Field Producer: Person who assists reporter and videographer when they're on an assignment. Makes interview appointments, helps gather information and manages/coordinates newsgathering activities from remote locations.

File: To present a report. Can be used to describe a place where information is stored (i.e., computer files, file folders).

Fill Copy: News stories that are not expected to be aired but could be used to complete a newscast that is running unexpectedly short.

Freeze Frame: A single frame or scene from a *videotape, digital tape* or *digital* image that can be locked in and shown to viewers. Also called a *still frame* or *still store*.

Graphic(s): *Visual* material that appears on the television screen. Examples: pictures, slides, charts, *supers, still frames* and other electronically generated images.

Handout: Source material provided to a news organization by a company, agency, group, etc. Also called a *news release* or *press release.*

Hard News: Reports of timely and significant events and issues.

Hit: An individual *live shot.* For example, a reporter might say she did hits from the fire at 4:30, 5:00 and 5:30.

IFB: Short for "interrupted feedback." It's the electronic system that permits a newscaster or reporter doing a *live shot* to hear technicians, *producer*s and directors. Also can refer to the earpiece used by reporters and newscasters during live broadcasts.

In: Short for *incue.*

Incue: First three or four words of an *actuality, soundbite, voicer, wraparound* or *reporter package.*

Intro: Introduction. *Copy* for newscaster to read to introduce actualities, *soundbite*s, *voicer*s, wraparounds, *package*s or other video-enhanced stories.

Jump Cut: Abrupt switch from one video scene of main action to another. Second scene contains people and things that appear in the first scene, but people and/or things have changed position or are doing something different. A noticeable "jump" in the flow of the video is the result. Normally, jump cuts should be avoided.

Key: Short for *chromakey.*

Kicker: Final story of a newscast—often humorous and/or unusual. Designed to leave audience members with a good, upbeat, positive feeling.

Lead: First sentence or two of a news story. Designed to grab audience interest and let them know what the story is going to be about. Can also refer to the first story in a newscast.

Lead-in: Introduction to an *actuality, soundbite, voicer, wraparound* or *reporter package.* See *Intro.*

Lineup: List of stories and other material in the order they are to be used in a newscast. Also called a *rundown.*

Liver: A live interview in the studio or from the field. Pronounced "leyever."

Live Shot: Airing news events, interviews or reporter *stand-up*s as they occur from a remote location away from the studio/station. Also called a *liver.*

Long Shot: See *Cover Shot.*

Look Live: A recorded story or news segment that is made to look as if it's being done live.

Matched Action: Editing video so that action in a scene is matched with a *close-up shot* of the same action in the very next scene. Designed to give the impression that two cameras were used to capture the video in a seamless, continuous manner.

Matched Cut: See *Matched Action.*

Matching Point: Scene in video that requires precise coordination with narration by a newscaster or reporter. Audience members MUST hear about what they're seeing at the precise time the scene appears. A matching point normally occurs the first time a major person, place or thing appears in video.

Medium Shot: Video scene that contains a somewhat limited amount of material. Usually restricted to fewer than three people. Camera approximately 8–12 feet from action.

Narration Track: *Copy* recorded by a reporter for a *voicer, wraparound* or *package.* Also called a *voice track.*

Nat Pkg: Short for *natural package.*

Nat Sound: Short for *natural sound.*

Natural Package: A story where the *anchor* reads a script to go with *nat sound* video and *soundbite*s. Much like a *VO/SOT.* Also can be a story that has no reporter/*anchor* narration, just *nat sound* and *soundbite*s.

Natural Sound: See *Background Sound.*

Newscast Director: Person responsible for the technical aspects associated with getting a live television newscast on the air. Directs the efforts of the technicians and engineers who work in the master control room.

Newscaster: See *Anchor.*

News Director: Person in charge of the news department. Oversees day-to-day newsroom operations. Hires and fires. Responsible for budget. Works with station management.

Newser: A news conference.

News Release: Information sheet from a business, institution or agency. Usually has a public relations function. Also called a *press release.*

Non-linear Editing: Using computers and *digital* technology to edit a story. Shots can be added or deleted easily at any place within the story without having to re-edit the entire *piece.*

On-air Person: See *Anchor.*

On-air Personality: See *Anchor.*

One-man Band: A reporter who, in addition to gathering information, writing and creating a *voice track*, also shoots and edits the accompanying video to create a complete, ready-to-air story.

One-on-One: Newscaster or reporter interviews a newsmaker without other newscasters or reporters present.

Open: Standard beginning music and/or announcer portion of a newscast.

OTS: Short for "over the shoulder." Usually used in connection with some sort of *graphic* or video scene inserted/shown "over the shoulder" of an *anchor* person.

Out: Short for *outcue.*

Outcue: Final three or four words of an *actuality, voicer, wraparound* or *reporter package.*

Out Take(s): Audio or video material that is recorded, but not included in aired versions of stories.

PA: Short for *production assistant.*

Package: Short for *reporter package.*

Pad Copy: See *Fill Copy.*

People Story: Story that focuses on a person or group of people. A "humanistic" approach to coverage of an event or issue.

Personality: See *Anchor.*

Personality Feature: Story that focuses on an aspect of the life and times of one person. Sometimes called a *personality profile.*

Personality Profile: See *Personality Feature.*

Phoner: A story aired by a reporter using a telephone.

Piece: A story or newscast *feature.*

Press Release: See *News Release.*

Producer: Person responsible for the content and organization of a newscast.

Production Assistant: Person who assists newscast *producers* and/or a *newscast director*. Often will help sort scripts, work with technical equipment, run errands, make appointments and greet guests.

Promo: See *Bump*. Usually refers to *copy* that is read and/or video that is shown during commercial breaks associated with non-news programming. Designed to entice audience members to watch an upcoming newscast.

Prompter Copy: *Copy* prepared for a *teleprompter*.

Pronouncer: A phoneticized guide to help a newscaster pronounce a word or name correctly.

PSA: Short for "public service announcement." Material provided by or prepared in support of non-profit organizations or community groups that is aired free by radio and television stations.

Q & A: Short for "question and answer." See *Crosstalk*.

Reader: News story that a newscaster reads without actualities, *soundbite*s or video. May include the use of *chromakey graphics*.

Reader-Act: Short for *reader* and *actuality*. See *Actuality Story*.

Remote: A *live shot* or segment. Reporting crew files material from a "remote" location away from studio/station.

Reporter Bridge: *Stand-up* used as a transition between story aspects or locations.

Reporter Package: News story in which reporter narration is coupled with recorded comments from news sources. Video used in *package*s for television news.

Rip-and-Read: Reading *wire copy* on air without rewriting it.

Rollcue: Predetermined word or words that serve as a cue to the *newscast director* to roll video. Most often used during live reports. For example, a reporter is on camera giving information about a fire. When he says the "rollcue" of "fire trucks arrived...," the director rolls pre-edited video of the trucks arriving. Viewers continue to hear the reporter, but see the fire trucks and the subsequent video.

Rolling Hit: Reporter previews a story live while on the way to cover the story.

ROSR: Short for "radio on scene report." A live or recorded report from the scene of a news event. Reporter describes what he or she sees, hears and/or does. Much like an eyewitness account.

Round Robin: A series of related news stories that air back-to-back. A newscaster introduces the first story, but until the entire segment is completed, reporters handle the transitions between stories without returning to the newscaster. Reporter A tosses to reporter B, reporter B tosses to reporter C and so on. Also called *team coverage*.

Rundown: See *Lineup*.

Satellite Coordinates: Specific location/position where satellite signals can be found.

Scener: Reporter sets the scene for a story or an information-gathering opportunity just before the action/activity begins. A type of "preview of coming attractions." Examples: A preview of what's likely to be talked about at an upcoming news conference; a preview of what is scheduled to take place during an impending special event.

Set: Desk, related furniture and background where news, sports and weather *anchor*s deliver the news.

Set Piece: TV reporter appears on the news *set* during a newscast to present a story.

Shot List: Chronological order of individual video scenes in the final edited version of a video story.

Signature Line: Final sentence or two spoken by a reporter in a *package*, *voicer* or *wraparound*. Used for identification purposes. Usually includes the geographic location of the events, the reporter's name and the *call letters* of the station. Example: "From North Midcity, I'm Terry Kegel for KCTI News." Also called a *tag line* or *sign off*.

Sign Off: See *Signature Line*.

Silent-sound: Television news story that combines an *anchor voice-over* and a *soundbite* or full-volume *natural sound*. Also called a *VO/SOT* or *studio package*.

Slug: Abbreviated title or summary for a story. Usually one or two words. Often placed in upper left or right corner of news script. Example: Tax Hike.

SNG: Short for "satellite news gathering." Use of satellites and related technologies to gather and report the news.

Soft News: *Feature* stories that usually are timeless. See *Feature.*

SOT: Short for "sound on *tape.*" Sound recorded in sync with picture on *videotape* or *digital tape.*

Soundbite: Recorded comments from a news source. Usually, only the news source is seen in the video. Often used as a synonym for *actuality* in radio.

Soundpop: See *Soundbite.*

Source Copy: Material used as a basis for writing or rewriting a story for air. Examples: *wire copy*, newspapers, *news releases* and reporters' notes.

Spot: Radio or television commercial.

Spray the Scene: Videographer shoots cover video of an event or location.

Stand-up: Story segment where reporter is seen speaking directly to camera.

Stand-up Close: *Stand-up* used to end a *reporter package.*

Stand-up Open: *Stand-up* used to begin a *reporter package.*

Stand-upper: Entire story presented as an extended *stand-up.*

Still Frame: See *Freeze Frame.*

Still Store: See *Freeze Frame.* Also refers to the process of saving single frames/scenes of video or other *graphics* in a computer.

Stretch: Command given to newscaster or reporter when time needs to be filled prior to the end of a newscast or newscast segment. Usually results in *ad-libbing* or repetition of information.

Studio Package: Television news story voiced by newscaster. Includes video action and one or more *soundbites.* Also called a *VO/SOT.* Can also refer to bringing a reporter into the studio to do a story during a newscast.

Super(s): Letters, numbers and words superimposed on a television screen by a *character generator.*

Switcher: Machine used to select the studio camera shots and other video material that will be seen by viewers. It permits "switching" from one *visual* source to another.

Tag: Ending sentence or two that an *anchor* reads following an *actuality, wraparound, soundbite, voicer, VO/SOT* or *reporter package.*

Tag Line: See *Signature Line.*

Tail: See *Tag.*

Talent: See *Anchor.*

Talking Head: See *Soundbite.* Usually only the head and the top of the shoulders of the news source are seen. Sometimes used as a synonym for a TV *reader* story when only the head and top of the shoulders of the newscaster are seen on screen.

Tape: *Audio tape, videotape* or *digital tape.*

Tape Cut: An *actuality* or *soundbite.*

Team Coverage: Multiple reporters and videographers cover different aspects of a story. Usually done in connection with major, *breaking news* stories.

Tease: See *Bump.* Also "teaser."

Teaser Lead: *Lead* that "teases" audience members into paying attention because it leaves out important information that will be revealed later in a story. Also "suspended interest lead."

TD: Short for *technical director*.

Technical Director: Person who assists the director of a newscast

Teleprompter: Device that allows television newscasters to read *copy* without having to look away from the studio camera lens. Mirrors or electronics used to reflect words over the front of the camera lens.

Toss: See *Bump*. Also refers to comments that one *on-air personality* makes to another right before the other *personality* begins speaking. A transition between *anchors*.

Total Running Time: Length of entire story from first word to last word, including the *intro* and *tail*, plus all actualities, *soundbites*, *voicers*, *packages*.

Track: Short for *narration track* or *voice track*.

TRT: Short for *total running time*.

Upper: Short for *stand-upper* or *stand-up*.

Video Journalist: News staffer who functions as both the reporter and videographer on a story.

Video News Release: Complete video story, *soundbites* or *B-roll* sent to TV news departments by companies, organizations or agencies. Usually serves a public relations function.

Videotape: Magnetic *tape* used to record sound and picture in sync.

Virtual Set: A *digital* news *set* that permits the easy use of a variety of *visual* backdrops and other effects.

Visual(s): See *Graphic(s)*. Material used to enhance a story. Examples: pictures, slides, *supers*, *videotape*, *digital tape* or electronically generated *graphics*.

VJ: Short for *video journalist*.

VNR: Short for *video news release*.

VO: Short for *voice-over*.

Voice-over: Television story in which a newscaster reads *copy* while video is seen by the audience. Usually includes *natural sound*.

Voicer: Radio news story introduced by a newscaster but narrated by a reporter live or pre-recorded. Usually does not contain actualities.

Voice Track: See *Narration Track*.

VO/SOT: Short for "*voice-over*/sound on *tape*." A *voice-over* combined with a *soundbite* from a news source. See *Silent-Sound*. Pronounced "V-O/S-O-T" or "Voh/Saht."

Wallpaper Video: See *Eyewash Video*.

Wide Shot: See *Cover Shot*.

Wild Sound: See *Background Sound*.

Wire Copy: News stories provided over computer networks by the Associated Press (AP), Reuters and others.

Wrap: Short for *wraparound*. Also *wrapper*.

Wraparound: Radio *reporter package* that combines one or more actualities or *soundbites* sandwiched between segments of reporter narration. The reporter's voice is "wrapped around" the actualities.

Wrapper: See *Wraparound*.

PART 1

Writing the Story

▶ REWRITING

Be Original

As a radio-TV newswriter, it's mandatory that you understand the material and information you're writing about before you start writing. A great deal of radio-TV newswriting is actually rewriting—rewriting wire copy, news releases, scripts and handwritten notes.

Whatever information source you use, the important thing is to understand it. If you don't understand it, how can you hope to write a story that your audience members will understand? Look for the basic elements of journalism—the who, what, where, when, why and how. They'll help you begin to organize your story.

A good practice is to read over the source copy a couple of times, put it aside, and try to tell the story to another person or say it to yourself. After you've done that, then go ahead and start writing.

Try not to look back at the source copy. Tell the story in YOUR OWN WORDS, not someone else's. Every other radio station, television station and newspaper in your community will more than likely create stories using the same material. You want your story to sound different from all the others. The only way to do that is by telling the story in YOUR words.

Don't simply retype, rearrange or "cut and paste" the words and sentences used in the source copy. Tell the story in your own words. You can make it more conversational and easier to understand. Your version doesn't always have to be *better* than the original, but it should always be significantly *different* from the original.

> **Example: (Original):** A violent crime surge in three U.S. cities has prompted the Justice Department to dispatch special anti-crime teams of federal agents to combat gangs and spiking murder rates in Phoenix, Ariz., Miami, Fla. and Riverside, Calif. The violent crime wave in the three cities contributed to the 1.5% rise in violent crime nationwide last year—an increase for the third straight year.

> **Example: (Rewrite):** Violent crime in the U-S is up again . . . for the third straight year. Violent crime spikes in three cities . . . Phoenix, Arizona, Miami, Florida and Riverside, California . . . contributed to the one-point-five-percent increase last year. The Justice Department is sending special anti-crime teams to those cities to help reduce gang violence and murders.

▶ SHORT, LEAN SENTENCES

Short but Sweet

One way to improve source copy is to shorten the sentences. A good average length for radio-TV news sentences is about 20 words. But avoid the choppy and stilted style of "See Spot run. Run, Spot, run." Create a flow and rhythm to your copy—a natural, conversational flow and rhythm. Sentences should flow easily without abrupt changes in topic and without awkward pauses and phrasing.

Alternate long sentences with short ones. Alternate the simple declarative sentences with sentences starting with *and, but* or *because*. People talk this way, so you should write this way. As long as it *sounds* okay and as long as it's conversational, use it.

The subject-verb-object sentence is best for clarity and directness. Stay away from clauses and phrases that sound unnatural. Not many people start a sentence with a phrase. It just doesn't sound right.

Example (poor): Speaking before a group of Midcity University students, State Senator Sam Bergman today announced his candidacy for governor.

Does the above example sound natural to you? Probably not. You don't talk that way, so don't write that way.

Example (better): State Senator Sam Bergman told a group of Midcity University students today that he's going to run for governor.

Remember, write the way you talk.

Trim the Fat

Write lean sentences, NOT fat sentences. A lean sentence is one that's trimmed of all excess words, especially adverbs and adjectives and other qualifiers that can distort what happened or what was said. Let your verbs provide the action and the color in your writing.

Avoid such words as *beautiful, ugly, hurriedly, slowly, frantically, lazily, smug, excitedly, happy, sad, good* and *bad*. This doesn't mean your writing has to be stripped down to the bone. Just avoid the "value judgment" adverbs and adjectives. Your judgments might not match those of your audience members.

Be accurate in your descriptions. If a woman wears a "red" dress, and you feel you must mention the dress, write she was wearing a "red" dress. Don't write she was wearing a "beautiful, flaming-red, exquisitely designed dress." What is beautiful, flaming and exquisitely designed to you might be ugly, dull and tasteless to someone else.

Example (poor): Looking fresh and excited, Mayor Gonzales walked quickly to the podium.

Example (better): Mayor Gonzales raced to the podium.

▶ BREVITY

Make It Brief

Time limitations are among the greatest handicaps to the radio-TV newswriter. Not only are you often on deadline, but you also must keep your stories to less than 30 seconds. You simply don't have enough time to write all you'd like to write about every story. You have to get to the news, explain why it's news, and give as many important details as possible in the limited time available.

You have to cut out all the frills and get right to the heart of each story. Be as brief and concise as you can while still including all the necessary facts.

Tight but Not Constricting

In your efforts to trim the fat from your story and to be brief, be sure you don't omit necessary detail. Don't sacrifice meaning for brevity. Don't distort or leave out what's essential.

You have to be an editor. Decide what is important for your audience members to know and share it with them. Don't forget to explain WHY things are important and WHY things happen. Point out the significance. Explain the meaning. Tell your audience members how events, issues and developments will affect them. Answer the question, "So what?"

Include the causes and results of events, issues, policies and statements. WHY are phone bills going up? WHY are the garbage collectors on strike? WHY is the economy in trouble?

Be sure to give your audience members the reasons behind actions. Include all the important details. Your job is to explain complex events in a concise manner using understandable language. Do a thorough, professional job.

▶ HELPING LISTENERS AND VIEWERS

One to a Customer

When you're trying to report the complete story, don't cram your sentences with a jumble of separate facts. The old "summary lead" works reasonably well for newspaper and magazine stories, but it's rarely appropriate for radio-TV news stories. Limit most of your sentences to one idea, fact or image. It can become confusing when you start crowding different concepts, facts and elements of a story into a single sentence.

Take each part of the story one step at a time—one sentence at a time. When you limit sentences to one main point each, you give your audience members a chance to hear and understand all the elements of the story.

When you pack your sentences with a number of points, your audience members are bound to miss some of them. Remember, listeners and viewers can't easily go back and relisten as readers can go back and reread something they miss or don't understand the first time.

In most situations, listeners and viewers have to get the information on the first shot, or they don't get it at all. Taking the elements of each story one at a time—a sentence at a time—gives your audience members the best chance of getting the information they should get.

Example (poor): Governor Bonner says he paid only 50-dollars in state income taxes last year, because he suffered heavy losses in the stock market and donated his gubernatorial papers to Midwest State University where officials set the value of those papers at more than 300-thousand-dollars.

Lots of separate facts have been crowded into that one sentence. So many, in fact, that it's hard to understand them all. A rewrite of Governor Bonner's tax problems could help simplify the issue.

Example (better): Governor Bonner says he paid only 50-dollars in state income taxes last year for two main reasons. First . . . he suffered heavy losses in the stock market. And second . . . he donated his gubernatorial papers to Midwest State University. The University estimates those papers are worth about 300-thousand-dollars.

Nickel and Dime the Audience

Another way to help your listeners and viewers understand all the elements of your story is to use simple and direct words—the "nickel and dime" words. The big, impressive-sounding, multisyllabic, "10-dollar" words don't belong in radio-TV newswriting.

"The simpler the better" should be your motto, because the simple words are the ones more people will understand. Take a look at the following list of words. See if you don't agree that the simple words are the better words for radio-TV newswriting.

Use	Don't Use
anger	indignation
send	transmit

buy	purchase
show	exhibit
need	require
cuts	lacerations
bruises	contusions
dead	deceased
try	attempt
enough	sufficient
home	residence
give	contribute
question	interrogate
see	witness
use	utilize

▶ TELL THE STORY

Talking It Out

While writing your story, it's a good idea to say the sentences out loud before you write them on paper or put them into the computer. If you talk your story out—or at least say it to yourself—and it sounds simple and understandable to you, it's a good bet that your audience members will understand it, too.

After you've finished writing your story, read it out loud. Listen to how it *sounds*. Be sure it says what you want it to say. Be sure you sound as if you're *telling* a story, not *reading* a story.

Example: Taxi service in Midcity is going green. Mayor Ronald Moore says over the next two years all of the taxi companies in town will have to convert to fuel-efficient hybrids. The phase-in will work like this: Within the next six months, 25-percent of all taxis will have to be hybrids. This time next year, 50% will have to be hybrids. Two years from now, all our taxis will be hybrids. In addition to being fuel-efficient, the taxis will have to be painted some shade of green to emphasize their environmentally friendly nature.

▶ READ THE STORY

Eyeing It Up

Although much of the emphasis in radio-TV newswriting is on writing copy that's easy on the ear, you should remember that somebody—you, a newscaster or a sportscaster—has to *read* that copy. You have to make your copy easy on the eye as well as easy on the ear. You'll need to follow the rules we've already covered, plus all the ones to come in Part 2.

A little later we'll be going over some specifics on how to write words and numbers so they're easy for a newscaster to read. We'll also cover how to provide pronunciation guides and how to edit a printed script.

The important thing to remember is to write your stories so the newscaster can read them easily and the audience members can listen to them and understand them easily.

Example: Midcity is getting a new, downtown library after all. The Board of Supervisors approved the 25-million-dollar project this morning. Last week, the Board voted to delay the project for at least five years, but Mayor Ronald Moore agreed to some budget modifications that freed up enough money to fund the new library. The new 80-thousand-square-foot library will be built on city-owned land at the corner of Broadway and Market. Construction is scheduled to start next month.

▶ SUMMARY

Here's a quick summary of the general hints for radio-TV newswriting that we've covered so far.

1. Be original. Tell the story in your own words. Don't parrot source copy.
2. Use short sentences, but create a flow to your writing—a natural, conversational flow.
3. Trim the excess fat of needless words, especially adjectives and adverbs.
4. Be as brief and concise as you can.
5. Write tightly, but don't sacrifice meaning. Be sure to include the WHY, the significance and the meaning of the story.
6. Don't cram your sentences full of facts. Take the elements of each story one at a time—a sentence at a time.
7. Use the "nickel and dime" words, not the "10-dollar" words. Use words that are easy to say, easy to listen to and easy to understand.
8. Talk your story out. Make sure it *sounds* right.
9. Make your stories easy on the eye as well as easy on the ear. Make it easy for a newscaster to read your copy and make it easy for your audience to listen to and understand your copy.
10. Think and write the way you talk.

PART 2

Using Radio-TV News Style

Did You Hear the One About . . . ?

Now that we've talked about radio-TV newswriting in general, it's time to get down to some specifics. Probably the most important part of a radio-TV news story is the first sentence or the first couple of sentences. If you don't get the attention of audience members at the beginning, all your fact gathering and all your careful writing will have been for nothing.

The first part of the story is called the *lead*. The lead should tell your audience members what the story is going to be about. It's kind of like a headline in a newspaper. It sets the tone of the story. It captures the flavor of the story. It characterizes the story.

The lead is what you'd say right after you met a friend. "Hi Jack, guess what happened today?" Or "Guess what I saw?" Or "Have you heard?" The THING that happened, the THING you saw, or the THING you heard is the lead.

Example: Jill, have you heard? Mayor Alvarez resigned today.

Example: Jack, guess what? All our teachers are on strike, so there's no school tomorrow.

Example: Jill, did you hear? Three people died in a plane crash at the airport this afternoon.

Example: Jack, did you hear the latest? The governor vetoed the tuition-hike bill.

Tell the most important part of the story right at the start. After you do that, the rest of the story should fall into place without too much trouble. Once you have the lead, fill in the details and explain the significance—what the story means and how it affects people.

Even though the lead of a radio-TV news story is often similar to a newspaper headline, it's not a good idea to use "headlinese" in your lead. Remember, write the way people talk. Strive for a natural, conversational flow in your writing.

Example (poor): Two die in street race.

Example (better): Two people died during a street race last night in South Midcity.

Example (poor): Supervisors sack Whittler.

Example (better): The Midcity Board of Supervisors fired City Attorney Edward Whittler this afternoon.

Example (poor): Former astronaut arrested in Florida kidnap caper.

Example (better): A former astronaut has been arrested and charged with kidnapping in Florida.

Example (poor): Governor wants minimum wage hike.

Example (better): Governor Sorenson wants to increase the minimum wage in the state.

Lead On

There are many different types of leads, but four of the most common are the emphasis lead, the umbrella or blanket lead, the verbless lead and the chronological or narrative lead.

Emphasis Lead

The *emphasis lead* is the one we've already talked about. You pick out the most important part of the story and emphasize it by using it at the beginning. It's generally the WHO, WHAT and WHEN of the story.

Example: Mayor Alvarez resigned this morning.

Mayor Alvarez is the WHO. *Resigned* is the WHAT. *This morning* is the WHEN.
Sometimes the WHERE of the story is one of the most important elements.

Example: An earthquake rocked Southern California this afternoon.

Example: Bombs hit London again this evening.

Example: A hurricane blasted Hawaii this morning.

Example: A brush fire is blazing out of control in East Midcity.

The WHY of most stories, although important, is usually saved for later in the story, because it often takes time to explain it fully. But be sure to include the WHY whenever you can.

Example (poor): Midcity Power says it's cutting back home heating oil allotments by 25-percent. That means about 20 gallons a month less for the average family.

Without the WHY, this story is incomplete. Listeners and viewers will want to know why the oil was cut back, so tell them.

Example (better): Midcity Power says it's cutting back home heating oil allotments by 25-percent. That means about 20 gallons a month less for the average family. The cutback is being blamed on a recent fire at a refinery.

Umbrella/Blanket Lead

The second type of radio-TV news lead is the *umbrella* or *blanket lead*. It's general instead of specific. It covers a number of things or a number of elements, but all of the separate parts are related in some way.

Example: The U-S Supreme Court ruled on three landmark cases this afternoon.

After you've let audience members know that you're going to be telling them about three things and not just one, you can start filling in the details.

Example: The U-S Supreme Court ruled on three landmark cases this afternoon. It decided that all the nation's obscenity laws are unconstitutional . . . that animals have legal rights . . . and that states can't require automobile license fees.

Do you see how an umbrella or blanket lead can group a series of separate but related stories into one neat package? A word of caution: Be sure all the stories belong under the same umbrella or blanket. Don't force the groupings. Avoid strange bedfellows.

Take a look at some good blanket leads.

Example: The Board of Education listened to lots of testimony, but took little action at its meeting this afternoon. (Follow with details of the debates and why there was no action.)

Example: Three major fires are raging out of control across the state this evening. (Follow with details about each fire.)

Example: Five Midcity people died in separate traffic accidents over the weekend. (Follow with the facts of each accident.)

Verbless Lead

The third type of radio-TV news lead is the *verbless lead*. It gets its name from the fact that no verb is used.

Example: Two more traffic deaths last night.

Example: A busy day at City Hall.

Example: More good weather in our future.

Verbless leads typically leave out "there were," "it was," "there is," and so on at the beginning of a sentence. While verbless leads can work well sometimes, use them sparingly. Complete sentences (subject-verb-object) are usually better, because that's the way we talk.

Chronological/Narrative Lead

The fourth type of radio-TV news lead is the *chronological* or *narrative lead*. You start with the first thing that happened and follow with the rest of the details in the order they happened.

Example: Tonight started out like any other night for Terri Anderson. She's the owner of the Thrifty gas station on Broadway. But about 9:00 o'clock . . . two men drove in . . . poked a gun in her ribs . . . and took all her oil. No money . . . just oil.

You probably won't use a narrative lead very often, but it is good for funny and/or lighthearted feature stories. Generally, you don't have enough time to give a chronological, blow-by-blow account, so start your story with information that would logically follow, "Guess what I just heard?"

No Questions, Please

An overworked, overused and unnatural-sounding lead is the *question lead*. You've probably heard millions of them.

Example: Are you tired and run-down?

Example: Do you suffer from chronic heartburn?

Example: Have you ever dreamed of owning your own business?

Example: Are you having money troubles?

Commercials use question leads all the time. You don't want audience members to think your story is going to be a commercial, so stay away from question leads. Besides, people tune to radio-TV newscasts for answers, not more questions. Your lead should answer the unasked but implied question, "Have you heard?"—not ask another question.

If you want a question-type lead, modify it for radio-TV news.

Example (poor): Are you looking for ways to save money on food? Well, we have some hints for you.

Example (better): If you're looking for some ways to save money on food . . . we have some hints for you.

Example (poor): Have you ever wondered what you'd look like with a smaller nose? A new computer program makes it possible.

Example (better): A new computer program makes it possible to see what you'd look like with a smaller nose.

Example (poor): Do you know where to find Peru on a map? About 80-percent of U.S. high school students don't.

Example (better): About 80-percent of U.S. high school students don't know where to find Peru on a map.

Turn to page 10 to compare some leads.

Choose a Lead #1

Now that we've gone over some of the ways to write radio-TV news leads, let's take a closer look at some examples. If you have an audio recorder handy, record the two leads on this page and play them back. If you can't record them, read them out loud and decide which one would be better for radio-TV news.

1. General Motors Corporation has announced that it is boosting retail price tags on its passenger cars by an average of 500-dollars because of increasing costs of steel and rubber.

2. General Motors is raising new car prices. The average increase is 500-dollars. G-M says it has to charge more because steel and rubber costs are up.

If you think the first lead is the better radio-TV news lead, turn to page 11.

If you think the second lead is better, turn to page 12.

So, you think the one long sentence is the better radio-TV news lead? Read it out loud.

General Motors Corporation has announced that it is boosting retail price tags on its passenger cars by an average of 500-dollars because of increasing costs of steel and rubber.

It's quite a mouthful, don't you think? And maybe just a little awkward? Is it the way you would tell it to a friend? Would you really say, "Hey, Jack, have you heard? General Motors Corporation has announced that it is boosting retail price tags on its passenger cars by an average of 500-dollars because of increasing costs of steel and rubber"?

You'd more likely say, "Hey, Jack, have you heard? General Motors is raising new car prices. The average increase is 500-dollars. Five-hundred-dollars . . . can you believe it? Everything is going up these days. I wish the price of steel and rubber hadn't gone up."

Of course, you can't always write the story exactly as you would tell it to a friend, but you can come close. Try to make your leads as conversational as possible. Remember *sound* is important. You're trying to write a lead that will *sound* good to people and that will be easy for them to understand.

Turn to page 12 and try two more leads.

Nice going. You picked the right one. The one long sentence has been broken up into three short, crisp sentences. Yet the flow is still there. It's easier to understand this way, and it *sounds* better. Remember, *sound* is important. Both leads are acceptable, but the meaning is clearer in the second one, and it's a lot easier on the ear.

Choose a Lead #2

Record or read the next two leads out loud and decide which one is the better radio-TV news lead.

1. The Teamsters walkout continues at five major supermarket warehouses. Union members have decided to ignore their union leaders and a court order.

2. Ignoring their union leaders and a court order, Teamsters members have continued their walkout at five major supermarket warehouses.

If you think the first lead is better radio-TV news style, turn to page 13.

If you think the second lead is better, turn to page 14.

All right. You're doing fine. The first lead is definitely the better of the two. It gives the important elements first—"the walkout is continuing." The two-sentence form is short and sweet. It's easy on the ear, simple, clear, direct and understandable. Keep up the good work.

Choose a Lead #3

Record or read the next two leads out loud.

1. The F-B-I is looking for the business agent of Aerocraft Leasing Company. One of the company's planes crashed in a Miami neighborhood last night, killing eight people, and F-B-I officials think the business agent could have prevented the crash.

2. The business agent for the Aerocraft Leasing Company, the operators of a plane that crashed in a Miami neighborhood last night and killed eight people, is being sought by the F-B-I today because bureau officials think he could have prevented the crash.

If you think the first lead is the better one, turn to page 15.

If you think the second lead is better, turn to page 16.

Bad choice. Remember, it's not a good idea to start a sentence with a descriptive clause or phrase. That's what happened here. "Ignoring their union leaders and a court order" is a phrase. If you hit audience members with something like this right at the start of the story, they won't know what you're talking about. What group is ignoring its union leaders and a court order?

While audience members are wondering, they'll probably miss the name of the union. Let people in on WHO is doing WHAT before you get into the circumstances.

Remember, you're trying to lead people by the ear through your story, so give them a break. Tell them what you know in a way they'll be able to understand. Take the time to think how you would tell the story to a friend. Would you really say, "Jill, have you heard? Ignoring their union leaders and a court order, Teamsters members have continued their walkout at five major supermarket warehouses"?

You'd probably say something like "the Teamsters walkout is still going strong at those five supermarket warehouses. Union leaders have told the workers to stop and so has the court, but they're still striking."

Now, turn back to page 13 and record or read the next two leads out loud. Choose the one that *sounds* more natural and conversational to you.

Correct. The first lead is the better of the two. It's clearer, more listenable and far more understandable than the second one.

Choose a Lead #4

Record or read the next two leads out loud.

1. Kevin Carlson and Mollie Smith were married this morning in Chicago by their U-S Army recruiting officer, who also is an ordained Methodist minister.

2. An unusual wedding in Chicago this morning. Kevin Carlson and Mollie Smith were married by their U-S Army recruiting officer. The recruiter is also a Methodist minister, so everything's legal.

If you think the first lead is better, turn to page 17.

If you think the second lead is better, turn to page 18.

No. Sorry. The second lead is really awful. It's not even an acceptable newspaper lead. Too much information is crowded into one long sentence. Didn't you get a little confused when you were listening to it or saying it out loud?

The long clause that helps describe the aircraft company really breaks up the continuity of the sentence. Remember, the simple subject-verb-object sentence is the best one to use. It's clear, direct and understandable.

Go back and take another look at the two leads again. Try starting each lead with "Hey, Jack, have you heard?" See which one *sounds* better to you.

You'll see that the first lead is the better radio-TV news style lead. It's more natural—more conversational. Remember, think the way you talk and write the way you talk.

After you've looked over the leads again, record or read the two leads on page 15 out loud.

This one's a little tricky, but you should have been able to decide which lead was the better one by using that good old "Hey, Jill" formula. Go back and try putting a "Hey, Jill, guess what . . . ?" at the beginning of each lead. See which one *sounds* more natural—more like what you'd really say.

One extra piece of advice: It's not a good idea to start out a radio-TV news story with an unknown name like "Kevin Carlson." Too many listeners will miss it. Try to ease audience members into a name. Tease the curiosity of your audience members first before hitting them with the names of the people involved.

Well-known names like those of your mayor, governor, U.S. senators, the president, professional athletes or movie stars are okay to put right at the beginning of the story—because people will recognize the names of celebrities—but little-known or completely unknown names should be used after you've grabbed the audience's attention.

Go back and reread the two leads on the army wedding. Then turn to page 18.

Good choice. The second lead is the better one for radio-TV news. The first sentence sets the listeners up for the information in the second and third sentences.

"An unusual wedding in Chicago this morning." The sentence sets the tone for the story. It tells audience members what the story is going to be about. It characterizes the story, and that's what a lead is supposed to do.

Remember, the lead is somewhat like a newspaper headline. It should NOT be written in "headlinese," but it should clue people in to what is coming up and it should attract their attention.

Try to write leads that would logically follow the opening, "Hey, did you hear?" If you can do that and make it *sound* natural and real, you're on your way to mastering the art of radio-TV newswriting.

We're going to leave leads for a while and go on to some other elements of radio-TV newswriting, but later we'll come back and give you a shot at writing some leads of your own.

▶ NAMES AND TITLES

What's in a Name?

Just about every story you'll write will have at least one name in it. Most of the time there will be several names. Be sure to keep all of the names straight and be sure to spell all of the names correctly. Include a pronunciation guide, if necessary, to ensure names will be pronounced correctly.

Nothing shoots down a newscaster's credibility more than botching up somebody's name. When audience members hear a name mispronounced—or worse, the wrong name—they begin to wonder how much of the rest of the information is wrong, too. In addition, you offend news sources when their names are mispronounced. They'll likely think twice about dealing with you and your station again.

Take the time to check the names of people making news. When they're local, you can call them up and ask about the correct spelling and pronunciation of their names. When they're national figures, sometimes the wire services will have a name advisory you can check. You also can call the local branch of the agency or organization that the person represents.

Remember to ask around the newsroom, too. You never know what some of your fellow workers might know unless you ask.

Sometimes you'll get stuck on the correct way to pronounce a word. Don't forget that the dictionary is a good source.

Be sure to include a pronunciation guide for difficult names, places and words. The guides should be placed in parentheses next to the correctly spelled name or word. The syllable in all capitals is the emphasized syllable.

Example: Kristin Kadooka (kah-DOH-oh-kah)

Example: insatiable (ihn-SAY-shuh-bull)

The *United Press International Broadcast Stylebook* pronunciation guidelines are in the Appendix.

Who Was That?

Names provide other problems for the radio-TV newswriter. Audience members aren't always paying close attention to what the newscaster is saying, so if you start a story with a relatively unknown name, a lot of people will miss it.

Give the half-listening listeners a break. Give them a little hint that you're going to throw a name at them. Start with the person's title if he or she has one, or give a little information about why a little-known person is suddenly in the news.

Example (poor): Peter Jones of Midcity won the World Kissing Championship last night. He said it was the most fun he'd ever had.

Example (better): A Midcity man won the World Kissing Championship last night. Peter Jones said it was the most fun he'd ever had.

The second example is called *delayed identification*. It's a technique used quite often in radio-TV newswriting. It's a good way to help audience members catch a person's name.

If Peter Jones has a title, you can start with it.

Example: State Senator Peter Jones won the World Kissing Championship last night.

Example: Councilman Peter Jones won the World Kissing Championship last night.

You also can use a person's title to create another form of delayed identification.

Example: The owner of a Midcity sporting goods store won the World Kissing Championship last night. Peter Jones said it was the most fun he'd ever had.

If Peter Jones is very well known it would be okay to start with his name because audience members would recognize it and it would serve to arouse their interest. But when the name is not very well known, or not known at all, start with a title or what has made the name newsworthy.

When a person is well known because of the government position he or she holds, it's usually okay on the first reference to use the person's title with the last name only, leaving out the first name.

Example: Governor Hernandez

Example: Senator Heftel

Example: Mayor Anderson

Example: President Bush

If it *sounds* okay to leave out the first name, leave it out. If it *sounds* better to leave the first name in, leave it in. Let your ear be your guide. Remember, though, except for well-known people, ALWAYS include full first and last name when you use a person's title.

Title Placement

In radio-TV newswriting, a person's title usually is placed BEFORE his or her name.

Example: The Director of Human Resources for Midwest Bank, Melissa Miller, is celebrating this morning.

Example: The Vice-President of Marketing for TIMCO, Roberto Sanchez, is stepping down.

Example: Midcity University President Lakeesha Rice is calling for major changes in the school's athletic department.

You can place a person's title after his or her name, but if you decide to do it that way, be sure you do it in a conversational manner.

Example (poor): Melissa Miller, the director of Human Resources for Midwest Bank, is celebrating this morning.

Example (better): Melissa Miller, who is the Director of Human Resources for Midwest Bank, is celebrating this morning.

Example (poor): Roberto Sanchez, the vice-president of marketing for TIMCO, is stepping down.

Example (better): Roberto Sanchez, who is the Vice-President of Marketing for TIMCO, is stepping down.

Example (poor): Lakeesha Rice, the president of Midcity University, is calling for major changes in the school's athletic department.

Example (better): Lakeesha Rice, who is the President of Midcity University, is calling for major changes in the school's athletic department.

Endless Titles

Some titles can get fairly long and involved. When you run into one of these, try to shorten it or break it up into smaller parts so you won't have to stick all of it in front of the person's name.

Example (poor): The vice-president of the Midcity Women for the Protection and Enhancement of the Female Image on Television, Lori McFadden, says her group will sponsor an "Awareness Fair" next Friday. She says more than 10-thousand women will take part.

Example (better): The vice-president of a local women's organization says her group will sponsor an "Awareness Fair" next Friday. Lori McFadden, of the Midcity Women for the Protection and Enhancement of the Female Image on Television, says more than 10-thousand women will take part.

You can probably come up with other ways of handling long, awkward titles. The important thing is to be sure to break up mouthful titles into digestible pieces.

First Names First

When you use any name, except that of a well-known government official, the initial reference should include both the person's first and last names. Later references should be made using only the person's last name. Do not use the courtesy titles of Mr., Mrs. or Ms. This rule applies to both men and women.

Example (poor): Police say Richard Roundtree is wanted in connection with several recent bank robberies. Mr. Roundtree was convicted of assault with a deadly weapon 10 years ago.

Example (better): Police say Richard Roundtree is wanted in connection with several recent bank robberies. Roundtree was convicted of assault with a deadly weapon 10 years ago.

Example (poor): Police say Rachel Roundtree is wanted in connection with several recent bank robberies. Ms. Roundtree was convicted of assault with a deadly weapon 10 years ago.

Example (better): Police say Rachel Roundtree is wanted in connection with several recent bank robberies. Roundtree was convicted of assault with a deadly weapon 10 years ago.

Never use a person's title with just his or her last name on subsequent references. After giving the title with the full first and last name on the first reference, use just the last name on all subsequent references.

Example (poor): Doctor Sharon Kim is the new president of the Midcity Unified School District Board of Education. Doctor Kim replaces Professor Donald Sneed. Doctor Kim says she wants to maintain most of Professor Sneed's programs, but she has some changes in mind, too.

Example (better): Doctor Sharon Kim is the new president of the Midcity Unified School District Board of Education. Kim replaces Professor Donald Sneed. Kim says she wants to maintain most of Sneed's programs, but she has some changes in mind, too.

Eliminate the Middleman

A middle name or initial is rarely used in radio-TV newswriting unless the name or initial has become associated with a person.

Examples: J. Edgar Hoover, P. T. Barnum, Edward R. Murrow, Edward G. Robinson, Billie Jean King, Michael J. Fox, Sarah Michelle Gellar, Howard K. Stern, Samuel L. Jackson, John F. Kennedy, Sarah Jessica Parker, Mary Tyler Moore

Try your hand at the name game on the next page.

The Name Game

Using correct radio-TV news style, where would you put the person's name in the following sentences? Check the appropriate blank.

A. The President of Nuvo Motors, Kenneth Warren, says his company is going out of business.

Where it is ___   Before the title ___   Leave it out ___

B. Maria Castro, a Midcity attorney, has been elected president of the National Sports Agents Association.

Where it is ___   After the title ___   Leave it out ___

C. Karen Murphy, the newly elected chairperson of the Midcity Realtor's Association, will speak at the luncheon.

Where it is ___   After the title ___   Leave it out ___

D. The chairman of the Senate Investigating Committee on Crime, Violence, Perversion, Obscenity, and Pornography, Joel Davis, is being investigated for income tax evasion.

Where it is ___   Before the title ___   Leave it out ___

E. The Governor of Western New Zealand, Leonard Theodore, will visit the United States in late April.

Where it is ___   Before the title ___   Leave it out ___

F. Ruby Thybo, the director of the Midcity Friends of Cats Society, is looking for volunteers.

Where it is ___   After the title ___   Leave it out ___

Check your answers on the next page.

Answers to the Name Game

A. Where it is. The title is short enough to come before the name.

The President of Nuvo Motors, Kenneth Warren, says his company is going out of business.

B. After the title. Remember, titles always come before the name if they're not extremely long and involved. This one is short enough to come before the name.

Midcity attorney Maria Castro has been elected president of the National Sports Agents Association.

C. After the title. This title is getting close to being too long, but it's not quite long enough, so put it before the name.

The newly elected chairperson of the Midcity Realtor's Association, Karen Murphy, will speak at the luncheon.

D. Before the title. This title is really too long to stick in front of the name. You could break it up by writing, "Senator Joel Davis, who is the chairman of the Senate Investigating Committee on Crime . . . ." Or you might write, "Senator Joel Davis is being investigated for income tax evasion. He's the chairman of the Senate Investigating Committee on Crime . . . ." However you do it, the important thing is to come up with a way of breaking up long, involved, awkward titles.

Senator Joel Davis, who is the chairman of the Senate Investigating Committee on Crime, Violence, Perversion, Obscenity, and Pornography, is being investigated for income tax evasion.

E. Leave it out. Is his name really that important? Does it add anything to the story? Why not use just the title only in the first sentence and use the name later in the story?

The Governor of Western New Zealand will visit the United States in late April.

F. After the title. Give the listeners a break. You don't want them to miss the name of such a warmhearted woman, do you? Put the title first so the listeners can anticipate the name.

The Director of the Midcity Friends of Cats Society, Ruby Thybo, is looking for volunteers.

If you missed more than two, you might want to go back and reread the section on titles. After you've done that, or if you missed two or less, go on to the next page.

▶ IDENTIFICATION

Identification Please

Using titles is a good way to help identify people. Titles help distinguish Councilman Joe Smith from Professor Joe Smith, Reporter Joe Smith, Police Officer Joe Smith, Firefighter Joe Smith and all the other Joe Smiths in your community. You want to be as specific in identifying people as possible.

You don't want to just say, "Joe Smith has been convicted of murder," when it's Professor Joe Smith who's been convicted. If you don't include the title—one of the things that makes one Joe Smith different from the other Joe Smiths—audience members might get confused. That not only could be embarrassing for all the innocent Joe Smiths, but it could lead to a libel suit against you and your station.

Example: Midcity University Biology Professor Lisa Miller died in the crash.

Example: A local sporting goods store owner, Lisa Miller, died in the crash.

Example: Midcity attorney Lisa Miller died in the crash.

Example: Doctor Lisa Miller died in the crash.

Example: Police say Lisa Miller, who operates a chain of clothing stores in Midcity, died in the crash.

▶ ADDRESSES

Home Sweet Home

Try to find out the titles of people in the news and use them in your stories. When you can't get a person's title, it's a good idea to include his address to help identify him.

Example: Joe Smith, who lives at 29–83 Dove Avenue, is the new spokesperson.

Example: Joe Smith, of 29–83 Dove Avenue, is the new spokesperson.

When you include an address, it lets audience members know it's the Joe Smith who lives at 2983 Dove Avenue who is involved and NOT the Joe Smith who lives at 6745 Mercer Drive.

Whenever you include an address, use the "who lives at" or the "of" prior to the street numbers and name. It *sounds* more conversational.

You don't have to include addresses for all of the people in every story, but when specific identification is required—as in a crime story, an accident, or a trial—or when you don't have a title for the person, it's a good idea to give the address.

You don't always have to give all the specifics of the address. You can give the part of town, the street name or a general block number. This technique helps protect a person's privacy.

Example: Joe Smith, of East Midcity, . . .

Example: Joe Smith, of Dove Avenue, . . .

Example: Joe Smith, of the 29-hundred block of Dove Avenue, . . .

► AGES

Age Gracefully

Many radio-TV newswriters like to use a person's age as part of the identification process. This practice can get a bit tedious, especially if your story has three or four names in it.

Include a person's age only if it is significant to the story or if you have no other means of identifying him or her. You'd probably want to mention a person's age if he were unusually young or old to be involved in whatever he's involved in, but using a person's age merely for identification purposes is not a good practice.

If you have a person's title and/or address, why use his age, too? When you have nothing you can use for identification except his age, then use it.

When you do need to use someone's age, use it with the first and last name and write it in one of the following ways:

Example: 47-year-old Arthur Lord

Example: Arthur Lord, who is 47-years-old, . . .

Example: Arthur Lord died today. He was 47-years-old.

NEVER place an age after a name, as is often done in newspapers, and NEVER use a person's age with his last name only.

Example (poor): Arthur Lord, 47, . . .

Example (poor): the 47-year-old Lord

It is acceptable to use a person's age in connection with his title or with what has made him newsworthy. In such cases, you might delay the person's name until the next sentence.

Example: A 29-year-old Midcity construction worker won 40-million-dollars in the state lottery last night. Stan Davis plans to keep on working, though.

Example: A five-year-old girl died this morning in a freak accident. Lisa Lynn Hunt fell off a swing and broke her neck.

► ATTRIBUTION

Who Says So?

Attribution is the "who says so" in radio-TV news stories. It's the source of the information. You report attribution just as you do in normal speech. Stop and think about how you tell a story to a friend.

Example: Jerry said we ought to go to the movies. But Gayle said she'd rather grab a burger. Mark said he wanted pizza. Finally, Courtney said we should go to "Nick's Place," so that's what we did.

See how all the attribution—the who says so—is always at the beginning, before what was said? That's the way attribution is reported in radio-TV newswriting—at the beginning—NOT dangling at the end of a sentence or plopped in the middle of a sentence as you've seen in newspapers.

Example (poor): "I've discovered a cure for cancer and it really works," Doctor Beverly Atwater said today.

Example (poor): "I've discovered a cure for cancer," Doctor Beverly Atwater said today, "and it really works."

Example (better): Doctor Beverly Atwater says she's discovered a cure for cancer that really works.

Don't you think the last sentence *sounds* better and more natural with the attribution at the beginning? Besides, with the attribution at the beginning of the sentence, audience members will know it's Dr. Beverly Atwater and not the newscaster who's discovered a cure for cancer.

It's important to let people know right at the start who says what. There are times in radio-TV newswriting when attribution is delayed, but at this stage in your career as a radio-TV newswriter, place attribution at the beginning of sentences—who says so BEFORE what is said.

Try your hand at Attribution Test #1 on the next page.

Attribution Test #1

Indicate where you would put the attribution in the following sentences. Check your answers on the next page.

A. Professor Jerry Nelson says the time has come for students to revolt.

Where it is ___   End ___ Middle ___

B. "Poverty is only a state of mind," Susan Lynn said.

Where it is ___   Beginning ___   Middle ___

C. Christmas, Ebenezer Scrooge says, is for humbugs.

Where it is ___   Beginning ___   End ___

D. "Nothing excites my husband more than a good war movie," Joyce Boyd said.

Where it is ___   Beginning ___   Middle ___

E. "Midcity is America's finest city," Supervisor Anita Liang said.

Where it is ___   Beginning ___   Middle ___

F. Professor Tim Wulfemeyer says this learning experience for beginning radio-TV newswriters is fantastic.

Where it is ___   End ___ Middle ___

G. We need a stronger military force, General Willard Williams reported, because the Chinese are developing a new missile.

Where it is ___   Beginning ___   End ___

Check your answers on the next page.

Answers to Attribution Test #1

A. Where it is.

Professor Jerry Nelson says the time has come for students to revolt.

B. Beginning.

Susan Lynn says poverty is only a state of mind.

C. Beginning.

Ebenezer Scrooge says Christmas is for humbugs.

D. Beginning.

Joyce Boyd says nothing excites her husband more than a good war movie.

E. Beginning.

Supervisor Anita Liang says Midcity is America's finest city.

F. Where it is.

Professor Tim Wulfemeyer says this learning experience for beginning radio-TV newswriters is fantastic.

G. Beginning.

General Willard Williams says we need a stronger military force because the Chinese are developing a new missile.

All the attributions should be put at the beginning of the sentences. Remember, the "who says so" in radio-TV news comes before what was said.

If you didn't get *all* the attributions at the beginning of each sentence, you should go back and reread the section on attribution.

Say It with *Says*

There seems to be a perpetual contest going on in radio-TV newswriting to see who can come up with the most synonyms for *says*. All you have to do is check the dictionary and you'll find lots of words that can be used for attribution.

Examples: declares, discloses, points out, demands, states, maintains, remarks, claims, exclaims, proclaims, insists

What's wrong with *says* or *said*? You don't have to use a different word each time you want to attribute something to somebody. *Claims, insists, discloses* and all the rest have a slight tinge of editorial comment to them.

Reports is the least offensive of all the synonyms for *says*, so if you feel the need to vary your words of attribution from time to time, use *reports*. *According to* is another acceptable alternative. Leave all the others to the paperback writers.

If a person promises or asks something, you can report that he *promises* or *asks* it. But if a person merely makes a statement—just says something—use *says*. NEVER use *stated*. It sounds too formal and unnatural.

▶ REPETITION

Repeat, Repeat, Repeat

Don't be afraid to repeat words. If the word is the *right* word, don't hesitate to use it—more than once, twice or even three times. If the word fits, write it.

Don't fall into the trap that many sportswriters do. No team ever *beats* or *defeats* another team any more. It *humbles, nips, blasts, bombs, pounds, rips, cages, knifes, trounces, blanks, squashes, trips, corrals* or *bashes* the other team.

You can take color and variety too far in your writing. Use the natural words, the conversational words. You don't always have to be looking up synonyms to be a good writer. Use the words that you would use if you were telling your story to a friend.

▶ QUOTES

Quotable Quotes

Direct quotes—the speaker's *exact* words—are a little hard to handle in radio-TV newswriting. Quotation marks don't do much good. They might tell the newscaster to change the inflection in his voice a little, but that's about it.

When you really want audience members to know that the words are the speaker's *exact* words, there are several ways you can do it. Whatever you do, NEVER use the old "quote, unquote" method. It *sounds* too stiff and formal.

Example (poor): Frank Merriwell says . . . quote . . . "Football builds men" . . . unquote.

If you want audience members to know that the words are the speaker's *exact* words, you can use "quoting from his exact words," "and we're quoting him," "as he put it," "as she expressed it," or "and these are her words."

Example: Frank Merriwell said . . . and we're quoting him . . . "Football builds men."

Example: Senator Steinberg says . . . and these are her exact words . . . "Anybody making more than 500-thousand-dollars a year should have to pay extra income tax."

Example: Police Chief Mario Soto said . . . and this is the way he put it . . . "Organized crime controls most of the local bars."

There are other ways of introducing direct quotations, but the important thing is to make sure audience members know the words are the speaker's and not yours. People can't see the quotation marks in your copy, so you have to come up with another way to let them know.

By all means, if you're going to quote somebody's *exact* words, quote the *exact* words. Quote full sentences, not parts or bits and pieces.

Example (poor): Igor Kranak said he never dreamed life could be . . . what he called . . . "such a wonderful merry-go-round."

Example (better): Igor Kranak said . . . and this is the way he expressed it . . . "I never dreamed life could be such a wonderful merry-go-round."

When you come across a long quotation, there's the problem of getting out of it—of letting audience members know you're through quoting a speaker. Some ways to do it are:

Example: That's what Anna Poynter said about (whatever).

Example: Those were Anna Poynter's exact words.

Example: That's the way Anna Poynter put it.

Example: Anna Poynter said . . . and we're quoting her . . . "I've never seen anything so horrible. The flames were everywhere. I tried to get into the house, but it was no use. I just couldn't make it. I wish I'd never let Edgar smoke in bed. If I would have made him quit, he'd still be alive." That's what Anna Poynter said about the fire that killed her husband and destroyed her home early this morning.

Close But No Cigar

You can see how direct quotes are difficult and awkward to handle. Unless the *exact* words are so colorful or are so unique as to warrant being quoted exactly, avoid using direct quotations.

Paraphrase and use the form, "So and so says such and such." You can keep the essence of what a speaker said without having to quote him exactly. If the exact wording of the quote is not all that important, unusual, descriptive or colorful, use an indirect quote—a paraphrase.

Those examples of direct quotes can be written as indirect quotes very easily.

Example: Frank Merriwell says football builds men.

Example: Senator Steinberg says anybody making more than 500-thousand-dollars a year should have to pay extra income tax.

Example: Police Chief Mario Soto says organized crime controls most of the local bars.

Example: Igor Kranak says he never dreamed life could be such a wonderful merry-go-round.

Example: Anna Poynter says she's never seen anything so horrible. She says she tried to get into the house, but the flames were everywhere. She says if she'd made her husband Edgar stop smoking in bed, he'd still be alive.

Usually you don't lose anything by paraphrasing. In fact, sometimes you can gain clarity and leave out needless words.

Quotations Test

Rewrite each of the following sentences twice: First as a direct quote—making sure audience members will know the words are the speaker's exact words—and second as a paraphrased quote. Check your rewrites on the next page.

1. "I think college basketball is becoming too commercialized," Midcity University Athletic Director Mark Wulf said.

   DIRECT QUOTE:

   . . . .

   . . . .

   . . . .

   PARAPHRASED QUOTE:

   . . . .

   . . . .

   . . . .

2. "I have decided to run for governor," State Senator Melissa Wang announced today, "because this state needs new leadership. For too many years we've been too content with old methods and old solutions, but now we need new methods and new solutions to meet the challenges ahead."

   DIRECT QUOTE:

   . . . .

   . . . .

   . . . .

   PARAPHRASED QUOTE:

   . . . .

   . . . .

   . . . .

   Check your answers on the next page.

Answers to Quotations Test

1. **Direct quote:**

Midcity University Athletic Director Mark Wulf says . . . and these are his exact words . . . "college basketball is becoming too commercialized."

2. **Direct quote:**

State Senator Melissa Wang said today . . . and we're quoting her exactly . . . "I've decided to run for governor because this state needs new leadership. For too many years we've been too content with old methods and old solutions, but now we need new methods and new solutions to meet the challenges ahead."

Any of the "exact words" phrases would be okay to use. The important thing is to let people know that the words are the exact words the source used.

1. **Indirect quote:**

Midcity University Athletic Director Mark Wulf says college basketball is becoming too commercialized.

2. **Indirect quote:**

State Senator Melissa Wang says she's going to run for governor. She says the state needs new leadership because for too long we've been using old methods and solutions to deal with our problems. Wang says we need new methods and solutions to deal with the challenges of the future.

There are other ways you could have handled the indirect quotes, but see how indirect quotes can cut down excess wording? They are usually clearer, too, so use them most of the time in your radio-TV newswriting.

▶ FACTS OR OPINIONS?

To Attribute or Not To Attribute

Sometimes it's difficult to know whether or not to attribute a statement or some piece of information. Generally, *facts* DO NOT need attribution, but *opinions* DO need attribution. When in doubt, however, let audience members know where you got your information.

The following sentences could air without attribution:

1. Hail pelted three Midwestern states today.
2. Two local men died in a small-plane crash this afternoon.
3. A Midcity judge is suing a local dry cleaning shop owner over a lost pair of pants.
4. The Midcity Magicians continue their winning ways.
5. The price of gasoline is up again.

The following sentences need attribution:

1. The fires were deliberately set.
2. The crash was caused by pilot error.
3. A Midcity judge has filed a frivolous lawsuit against a local dry cleaning shop owner over a lost pair of pants.
4. Poor coaching has contributed to the Midcity Magicians' losing streak.
5. The new project will bring in millions of dollars in new taxes.

Be sure to include attribution whenever a statement or piece of information:

1. Is clearly opinion and is debatable.
2. Implies blame.
3. Hasn't been proven to be true.
4. Might be controversial.
5. Might be questionable.

Keep these "attribution musts" in mind as you take the self-test on the next page.

Attribution Test #2

Indicate whether attribution is needed in the following sentences.

A. A hurricane ripped across Florida this morning.

Needed _____ Not Needed _____

B. Mayor Shelley should be recalled.

Needed _____ Not Needed_____

C. The Minnesota Vikings are the best team in professional football.

Needed _____ Not Needed _____

D. A jumbo jet has crashed at Midcity International Airport.

Needed _____ Not Needed _____

E. Lots of heated discussion at the Board of Education meeting this afternoon.

Needed _____ Not Needed _____

F. The oil companies create gasoline shortages so they can make higher profits.

Needed _____ Not Needed _____

G. The price of milk is up again.

Needed _____ Not Needed _____

H. If the bill passes, it will mean the end to freedom of speech.

Needed _____ Not Needed _____

I. The Tigers defeated the Yankees 4-to-3.

Needed _____ Not Needed _____

Check your answers on the next page.

Answers to Attribution Test #2

A. Not needed. Fact. Who would dispute it?
B. Needed. Opinion. Listeners will want to know who wants to recall the mayor.
C. Needed. Opinion. Controversial and questionable. Plenty of people would dispute it, too.
D. Not needed. Fact.
E. Not needed. This is a fact—at least as the reporter sees it. He or she attended the meeting and determined it to be true. If you checked "Needed," you really aren't wrong though. Some would argue that this type of statement should have attribution. Actually, very often the question of whether or not to attribute a statement boils down to judgment. Things aren't always clear cut. Use your best judgment, but keep in mind that facts DO NOT need attribution and opinions DO need attribution.
F. Needed. Opinion. Statement implies blame and certainly would be disputed.
G. Not needed. Fact.
H. Needed. Opinion. It's questionable, controversial and probably isn't true.
I. Not needed. Fact.

If you missed more than one, you should reread the section on attribution. After you finish checking over the attribution section, or if you missed one or none of the attribution questions, proceed to the next page.

▶ AIDING THE AUDIENCE

Half-Listening Listeners

The half-listening audience member is one of the facts of life in radio-TV news. Rarely does anyone listen to the radio or watch the news on television without a number of distractions. Kids are fighting or talking loudly; the dog is barking; a roommate, husband, wife, boyfriend, girlfriend or some member of the family is doing something or saying something.

A person could be driving, eating, studying, doing housework, preparing food, working on a project, reading, dreaming, surfing the Internet or just thinking about something else besides listening to the news that's coming from the radio or the television.

As a newswriter, you have to try to overcome these distractions and get the news to your audience members, no matter how preoccupied or inattentive they may be. We've already talked about some ways to gain people's attention by writing crisp, snappy leads and giving a person's title and the attribution at the beginning of the sentence.

There are some other ways that you can give the half-listening listeners a break. You can *repeat* the extremely significant parts of stories toward the end so listeners who missed them the first time can get them the second time around.

You can mention the place where the big fire has destroyed thousands of trees near the end of the story as well as at the beginning. Repetition has a place in radio-TV news if the information deserves more than one mention.

Example: Fire continues to rage out of control in the Williams National Forest in East Midcity. At least four-thousand acres and 10-thousand pine trees have been scorched. Firefighters don't expect to have the fire under control until early next week. The fire in the Williams National Forest in East Midcity started four days ago when a lightning strike ignited dried pine needles.

Another way to help half-listening audience members is to avoid the words *former* and *latter*. People aren't going to remember who was mentioned first and who was mentioned second. Besides, people can't go back and relisten for something they missed or forgot as readers can go back and reread. Instead of *former* and *latter*, just mention again the last names of the people involved.

Example (poor): The judge decided in favor of Michael Marlowe and Jacob Stein. The former collected 10-thousand-dollars and the latter picked up eight-thousand-dollars.

Example (better): The judge decided in favor of Michael Marlowe and Jacob Stein. Marlowe collected 10-thousand-dollars and Stein picked up eight-thousand-dollars.

Remember, try to give audience members a break. They have a lot of distractions, but they still want to get the news. It's your job to get it to them.

▶ CONTRACTIONS

Contractions Can't Hurt

Contractions are good for what ails so much of radio-TV newswriting style—stiffness and formality. How often do you say, "Jill *did not* want to go skiing"? Never? You'd probably say, "Jill *didn't* want to go skiing."

Don't be afraid to use contractions. You do all the time in your everyday speech, so why not use them in your radio-TV news copy? They sound natural and conversational, so use them when they're appropriate.

There are times when you should NOT use contractions. One is when you want emphasis.

Example: Governor Atkins says he will NOT call in the National Guard.

When you want that *not* to come through loud and clear, write it in. Don't cover it up by using *won't*. Make it stand out.

Another time you might not want to use contractions is when the severity or formality of the situation dictates a more formal communication style. For instance, in reporting a major disaster, it would be better to say "The number of deaths has NOT been determined," rather than "The number of deaths hasn't been determined."

Use your own judgment, but remember, in most cases it *sounds* better to say *didn't* instead of *did not, shouldn't* instead of *should not, won't* instead of *will not, we'll* instead of *we will*, and *they're* instead of *they are*.

Some other contractions you might use include:

haven't **for** have not	isn't **for** is not
couldn't **for** could not	wasn't **for** was not
you're **for** you are	it's **for** it is **or** it has
can't **for** cannot	they'll **for** they will
aren't **for** are not	doesn't **for** does not
wouldn't **for** would not	they've **for** they have
she's **for** she is	we're **for** we are

► PRONOUNS

Who's He?

Using personal pronouns is a good way to humanize your copy. Use *we, us, our, they, you, he, she* and *it* wherever you can. But remember, whenever you use a personal pronoun, be sure it refers to the appropriate noun—the one you're talking about.

Example (poor): Professor Marvin Jones helped Professor George Langley with the experiment. He's from Iowa State University.

Who is "he" in the example? Is it Jones or Langley? It's hard to tell from the way it's written. You can imagine the poor listeners when they hear something like this. They just shake their heads and wonder, "Who's he?"

Pronouns usually refer to the last noun used in a sentence or paragraph. In the example, that would mean the "he" refers to George Langley, but is that what you want? More than likely the "he" is supposed to refer to Marvin Jones. The point is, if you want to avoid confusion and misunderstanding, be careful when you use personal pronouns. Make sure they refer to the intended noun—the one you want.

Example (better): Professor Marvin Jones helped Professor George Langley with the experiment. Jones is from Iowa State University.

You Is Us

Another good way to humanize your copy is to use *we* and *us* and *our* instead of *you* and *your*. As a newswriter, you are a part of the community, not some impartial observer. News that affects your audience members affects you, too.

Example (poor): *Your* electric bills will be going up soon.

Example (better): *Our* electric bills will be going up soon.

Example (poor): *You're* in for a cold winter.

Example (better): *We're* in for a cold winter.

Let audience members know that you're an active, concerned member of the community. It will improve your credibility and popularity, plus it will help you communicate better.

▶ VERB TENSE

Now Is the Time

Radio and television are the media of the moment. They are the "what's happening now" media. You should use the present tense of verbs or the present perfect tense whenever you can to emphasize this sense of immediacy.

Use *says* instead of *said, has reported* instead of *reported*. This doesn't mean that you should abandon the past tense altogether, but use it sparingly to describe things that have taken place in the fairly distant past.

Example: Texas Governor Billy Ray Jones has died.

Example: Texas Governor Billy Ray Jones is dead.

Example: Texas Governor Billy Ray Jones died early this morning.

All of the above examples could be used, of course, but don't you think the first two sound a bit more timely and immediate? Avoid the past tense whenever you can, but use it when necessary.

Example: We *reported* last week that the price of eggs *was going* up . . . but now it *looks* as if we *had* our facts scrambled.

You probably noticed the mixing of verb tenses in the above example. That's perfectly okay to do in radio-TV newswriting. You can vary verb tenses in your sentences as long as the sentences make sense. Varying verb tenses can help break up monotony.

Example: The Defense Department *has issued* a warning to Iraq. It *says* if the Iraqis *don't permit* on-site inspections, the U-S *will suspend* all humanitarian-aid projects. Iraqi leaders *had* no comment.

As long as the sentence *sounds* right, you're okay. Just make sure that when the sentence is read out loud, it makes sense.

▶ TIME ELEMENTS

Timely Time

When you use the past or future tense, you'll probably want to include the time element of the story—WHEN the story happened or WHEN it will happen. WHEN the action happened or will happen is often an important element, but you don't want to say "today" in every story. You'll bore audience members and yourself.

Try to be specific in your use of time. Use *this morning, this afternoon, this evening, minutes ago, just before we came on the air,* or whatever you can to convey as closely as possible the exact time of the event.

Example: We have breaking news. A brush fire is burning out of control in West Midcity.

Example: An earthquake rocked Southern California just moments ago.

Example: Robbers hit two local banks this afternoon.

Example: The meeting will start at 7:00 this evening.

Example: Local freeways are a mess this morning.

Natural Time

Avoid the awkward placement of the time element in the sentence. Place it where it *sounds* most natural. Usually, it's best to place the time element right before or after the verb. It's often placed at the end of the sentence. If you put it at the beginning of the sentence, you give added emphasis to it.

Example (poor): U-S Treasurer Doris Williams this morning resigned after a meeting with her lawyer.

Example (better): U-S Treasurer Doris Williams resigned this morning after a meeting with her lawyer.

Example (better): This morning, U-S Treasurer Doris Williams resigned after a meeting with her lawyer.

Example (better): U-S Treasurer Doris Williams resigned after a meeting with her lawyer this morning.

A time element often sounds awkward when it's used with a present tense or present perfect tense verb, but a time element does flow naturally out of a past tense or future tense verb.

Example (poor): Joe Sparr *says* this morning that he's giving up boxing.

Example (poor): Joe Sparr *has said* this morning that he's giving up boxing.

Example (better): Joe Sparr *said* this morning that he's giving up boxing.

As with so much else in radio-TV newswriting, when it comes to placing the time element in the sentence, let your ear be your guide.

▶ VERB VOICE

Action Please

Another thing to remember when you're selecting a verb is to use the active voice instead of the passive voice. A good, strong active voice verb will usually get across your meaning better than a passive voice verb.

Example (poor): The dog *was bitten* by the man.

Example (better): The man *bit* the dog.

Example (poor): Fire officials say the fire *was caused* by a short circuit.

Example (better): Fire officials say a short circuit *caused* the fire.

Example (poor): Midcity University *has been given* a five-million-dollar grant by the Albert Parvin Foundation.

Example (better): The Albert Parvin Foundation *has given* a five-million-dollar grant to Midcity University.

You can use the passive voice sometimes, but keep it to a minimum. It slows down the pace of your story and robs it of life and pep. Most of the time use the simple declarative sentence (subject-verb-object). It's the best. You can easily change a passive-voice sentence to an active-voice sentence by taking the object of the preposition and making it the subject of the sentence.

Example (passive): The bill was passed 55-to-45 by the Senate.

Example (active): The Senate passed the bill 55-to-45.

Example (passive): Johnson was appointed to the commission by Governor Gutierrez.

Example (active): Governor Gutierrez appointed Johnson to the commission.

Example (passive): The award was presented to Britney Worth by Caitlynn Parker.

Example (active): Caitlynn Parker presented the award to Britney Worth.

Example (passive): The plane's takeoff was delayed by fog.

Example (active): Fog delayed the plane's takeoff.

Example (passive): Murphy was found guilty by the jury.

Example (active): The jury found Murphy guilty.

The rewriting test on the next page gives you an opportunity to practice correct radio-TV newswriting.

▶ REWRITING TEST

Here's a chance for you to see how well you've understood the sections covering contractions, personal pronouns, verb tenses, verb voices and time elements. Rewrite each of the following sentences using correct radio-TV news style.

A. State Senator James Miller today has decided to sue columnist George Wilson. He has accused him of slander.

B. Councilwoman Marilyn Munson said she has not accepted campaign contributions today because she believes they are inappropriate.

C. The winning run was driven in by Reggie Norton.

D. Looks as if you will be paying more for light bulbs soon.

E. The final two spots went to Mary Flint and Mike Harrison. The former is a native of Philadelphia, Pennsylvania, and the latter is from Mason City, Iowa.

F. This afternoon fire has destroyed the Mueller Antiques store on Broadway. The fire was caused by faulty wiring, said fire officials.

Check your answers on the next page.

Answers to Rewriting Test

A. **Rewrite:** State Senator James Miller has decided to sue columnist George Wilson. Miller has accused Wilson of slander.

Drop *today*. Replace *he* with *Miller* and *him* with *Wilson*. Remember, keep your personal pronouns straight and avoid the awkward and needless use of a time element.

B. **Rewrite:** Councilwoman Marilyn Munson says she hasn't accepted campaign contributions because she believes they're inappropriate.

Change *said* to *says*. Change *has not* to *hasn't*. Change *she is* to *she's*. Change *they are* to *they're*. Drop *today*. Remember, use the present tense of verbs and contractions whenever possible. Plus, be sure to place the time element where it sounds most natural and if you don't need a time element, drop it.

C. **Rewrite:** Reggie Norton drove in the winning run.

Change the passive voice verb *was driven in* to the active voice verb *drove in*. Make *Reggie Norton* the subject of the sentence. Remember, use active verbs whenever possible. They make your sentences livelier.

D. **Rewrite:** Looks as if we'll be paying more for light bulbs soon.

Change *you will* to *we'll*. Use contractions, plus remember that you're in the same boat as your audience members. You is us, they are we, and your is our.

E. **Rewrite:** The final two spots have gone to Mary Flint and Mike Harrison. Flint is from Philadelphia, Pennsylvania, and Harrison is from Mason City, Iowa.

Change the past tense *went* to the present perfect tense *have gone*. It makes the copy sound a bit more timely. Replace *former* with *Flint* and *latter* with *Harrison*. Remember, NEVER use former and latter. Audience members can't go back and find out who was the former and who was the latter. Use the names again. You'll be helping the half-listening listeners.

F. **Rewrite:** Fire destroyed the Mueller Antiques store on Broadway this afternoon. Fire officials say faulty wiring caused the fire.

Change *has destroyed* to *destroyed*, so you can use the time element. Move the time element to the end of the sentence. Move the attribution to the beginning of the sentence. Make the second sentence active voice by changing *was caused* to *caused* and making *faulty wiring* the subject of the sentence. Remember, place time elements where they sound the most natural and avoid the use of time elements with the present perfect tense of verbs. In addition, keep your sentences in the ACTIVE voice whenever you can.

You can rewrite all of the sentences in other ways, of course, but if you missed three or more of the changes, you'd better go back and reread the sections. You need to master all of the concepts to be an effective radio-TV newswriter.

After you reread the sections, or if you missed less than three, go on to the next page.

► ABBREVIATIONS

What Does T-H-A-T Stand For?

The use of abbreviations in radio-TV newswriting can generally be summed up in three words: don't use them. Give the person who is going to be reading your copy on the air a little consideration. He or she might have trouble translating an abbreviation into words.

You yourself might even forget if you're reading your own copy on the air. Play it safe. SPELL OUT words so they look the way you want them to be read. Never abbreviate the names of states, countries, days of the week, months, government titles, religious titles, military titles, address designations or the words *junior* or *senior*.

Some abbreviations, such as Mr. and Mrs. and U.S., are so recognizable they're safe to use, but generally it's best to write out the word.

Examples (poor): Calif., N.Z., Wed., Nov., Gov., Rev., Sgt., St., Dr., Blvd.

Examples (better): California, New Zealand, Wednesday, November, Governor, Reverend, Sergeant, Street, Drive (or is it Doctor?), Boulevard

Organized Organizations

The names of most organizations should be written out completely the first time they appear in a story. Every additional reference can be made with the initials or a shortened version of the name.

Example: People Opposed to Pornography . . . known as POP . . . is at it again. POP members are burning all the dirty books they can find.

The same method can be used even if the group's name doesn't reduce to a neat acronym like POP.

Example: The Iowa Highway Patrol is cracking down on speeders. The I-H-P's new "get-tough" policy starts on Monday.

Some groups have become so well known by their abbreviated names that it's okay to use them without giving the full name first.

Example: Young Men's Christian Association is the YMCA (Y-M-C-A).

Example: National Aeronautics and Space Administration is NASA (NA-suh).

There are others, but make sure you're not taking too much for granted by using the abbreviated form of an organization's name. When in doubt, give the full name of the organization the first time you mention it in a story. Don't forget to include a pronunciation guide for the abbreviated name. Newscasters will appreciate it.

A R-O-S-E Is Not a ROSE

You might have noticed the hyphens between I-H-P and Y-M-C-A, but the lack of hyphens between NASA and POP. In radio-TV newswriting you use hyphens between letters and numbers that you want pronounced separately.

Example: Capitalize and place hyphens between U-N, U-S, F-B-I, I-O-U, T-N-T, C-I-A, C-B-S, N-B-C, W-O-I-T-V, G-O-P, N-C-A-A, N-double-A-C-P.

Example: The phone number is 2–9–2–1–7–5–9.

Example: The phone number is 2–9–2–17–59.

Example: He lives at 2–6–4–9 Sunset Street.

Example: He lives at 26–49 Sunset Street.

Example: She says 19–99 was a better year than 19–98.

Example: The 49ers won 14-to-6.

Example: The vote was 9-to-3 for acquittal.

Turn to the next page for Abbreviations Test #1.

Abbreviations Test #1

Look over each column and decide which one contains the correct radio-TV news treatment of abbreviations.

Column A	Column B	Column C
SOS	S-O-S	Save Our Ship
NCAA	N-C-double-A	Nat. Col. Ath. Assn.
294–4340	2-9-4-43-40	2944340
St.	Street	Strt.
Dr. Tim Wolf	Doctor Tim Wolf	Dct. Tim Wolf
Mister Jim Smith	Mr. Jim Smith	Mst. Jim Smith
1941	19-41	Nineteen-Forty-One
9865 North Ave.	9-8-6-5 North Avenue	9865 N. Ave.
Miz Grace Limbag	Ms. Grace Limbag	Mz. Grace Limbag
WHO-TV	W-H-O-T-V	Who-TV
Calif.	California	CA
Fri.	Friday	Fry-day
Eur.	Europe	Eupe
Lt. Jim Holtzman	Lieutenant Jim Holtzman	Ltnt.Jim Holtzman

If you think column A is the correct one, turn to page 46.

If you think column B is the correct one, turn to page 47.

If you think column C is the correct one, turn to page 48.

Column A? Not quite. Not one of the entries in column A is really acceptable radio-TV news style. Remember to spell out words completely and to place hyphens between letters and numbers that you want the newscaster to pronounce individually.

Go back and look at column B again. It's the correct way to handle abbreviations in radio-TV news. After you do that, turn to Abbreviations Test #2 on page 47.

Way to go! Column B is the correct radio-TV news style. Putting hyphens between numbers and letters that you want individually pronounced and spelling out the names of days, months, states, countries, addresses and most titles is the best way to ensure that what you want to say gets said.

Abbreviations Test #2

Rewrite the following sentences in correct radio-TV news style.

A. Jane Anderson has resigned from CBS and is now working for KOMU-TV, the NBC affiliate in Columbia, Mo.

....

....

....

B. Atty. Edward Whittler, 2347 E. West Ave., is a member of the NAACP.

....

....

....

C. LSU was defeated by BYU, 114-98.

....

....

....

D. Rev. J. J. Jefferson Jr. left the U.S. to live in the P.R.C. in 1993.

....

....

....

E. If you have any information, call 232-6677.

....

....

....

F. Lt. Thomas Forster says Sgt. John Riker is a hero.

....

....

....

G. Dr. Tim Kelly, 5491 Streeter Blvd., is the new Pres. of the Midcity YMCA.

....

....

....

Check your answers on page 49.

Column C is the worst of the three.

Go back and reread the section on abbreviations. Remember to spell out all words and to place hyphens between numbers and letters you want the newscaster to pronounce individually.

After you have reread the section, take another look at column B. It's the correct radio-TV news style. After you do that, do Abbreviations Test #2 on page 47.

Answers to Abbreviations Test #2

A. Jane Anderson has resigned from CBS and is now working for KOMU-TV, the NBC affiliate in Columbia, Mo.

A. **Rewrite:** Jane Anderson has resigned from C-B-S and is now working for K-O-M-U-T-V . . . the N-B-C affiliate in Columbia, Missouri.

B. Atty. Edward Whittler, 2347 E. West Ave., is a member of the NAACP.

B. **Rewrite:** Attorney Edward Whittler of 23-47 East West Avenue is a member of the N-double-A-C-P.

C. LSU was defeated by BYU, 114-98.

C. **Rewrite:** B-Y-U defeated L-S-U 114-to-98. (Did you remember to reverse the teams to avoid a passive voice verb? You could spell out *Brigham Young University* and *Louisiana State University*, too!)

D. Rev. J. J. Jefferson Jr. left the U.S. to live in the P.R.C. in 1993.

D. **Rewrite:** In 19-93, Reverend J-J Jefferson Junior left the United States to live in the People's Republic of China.

E. If you have any information, call 232-6677.

E. **Rewrite:** If you have any information, call 2-3-2-6-6-7-7 (OR 2-3-2-66-77). You decide how you want the anchor to read the numbers and use hyphens to indicate the desired pronunciation.

F. Lt. Thomas Forster says Sgt. John Riker is a hero.

F. **Rewrite:** Lieutenant Thomas Forster says Sergeant John Riker is a hero. (Did you spell *lieutenant* and *sergeant* correctly?)

G. Dr. Tim Kelly, 5491 Streeter Blvd., is the new Pres. of the Midcity YMCA.

G. **Rewrite:** Doctor Tim Kelly, of 54-91 Streeter Boulevard, is the new president of the Midcity Y-M-C-A. (Did you spell out *Doctor*? *5-4-9-1* would be okay instead of *54-91*. Did you spell *Boulevard* correctly?)

How'd you do? If you missed more than two, you'd better go back and reread the appropriate sections. After you've done that, or if you missed two or less, turn to the next page.

► NUMBERS

By the Numbers

Numbers provide some additional problems for the radio-TV newswriter. Numbers are hard to read aloud—especially long, involved numbers—so try to write numbers in a way that will help the newscaster read them easily. Here are some guidelines to follow.

For the single-digit numbers *one* through *nine*, write them out as words.

Examples: one, two, three . . . seven, eight, nine.

For the double-digit and triple-digit numbers *10* through *999*, use arabic numerals.

Examples: 10, 11 . . . 27 . . . 100 . . . 563 . . . 812 . . . 946 . . . 999

For all the rest of the numbers, use word-numeral combinations. Be sure to write out the words *thousand, million, billion, trillion*. Write out *hundred* only if the number is greater than one-thousand. A newscaster shouldn't have to think about or decipher numbers. Make them easy to read.

Be sure to include a hyphen between numbers and the words *thousand, million, billion, trillion*. Linking the parts of a number with hyphens keeps it together and helps ensure that a newscaster will read it correctly.

Examples: one-thousand, one-thousand-and-one, one-thousand-10, 11-hundred, 15-hundred, two-thousand, 26-hundred-25, 10-thousand, 100-thousand, 147-thousand-673, 999-thousand, one-million, one-million-217-thousand, 17-million-seven-thousand, 900-million, one-billion, 10-and-a-half-billion, 438-billion-six-million, 654-billion-339-million-146-thousand-272

Ban the Symbols

Don't use any *symbols* in radio-TV newswriting. SPELL OUT words like *dollars* and *cents*. Writing out a word instead of using a symbol makes it easier for the newscaster to read it.

Example: 123-dollars, **not** $123

Example: 10-cents, **not** 10¢ or $.10

Example: number, **not** # or No.

Example: percent, **not** %

Example: and, **not** &

When you're dealing with measurements or amounts, be sure to SPELL OUT words like *inches, feet, yards, miles, acres, meters, ounces, pounds, tons, pints, quarts, gallons, degrees*.

Examples: three-inches, 10-feet, 47-yards, 26-miles, 616-acres, 36-meters, 12-ounces, 255-pounds, 16-tons, two-pints, one-quart, 50-gallons, 72-degrees

Ordinary Ordinals

Use *st, nd, rd, th* after numbers used in dates, addresses and wherever else an ordinal is needed. We use our same number rules, of course. Single digits are written out as words. Double-digit and triple-digit numbers are written using numerals and the appropriate letter sounds.

Examples: first, June second, June third, Fifth Avenue, eighth, June 12th, June 21st, 29th place, 41st, 52nd time, 65th Street, 83rd, 110th, 221st, 333rd, 442nd

Bits and Pieces

Use our basic number rules for fractions and percentages. Remember to SPELL OUT the *point*, too.

Example: 12-point-five-million, **not** 12.5 million

Example: 12-and-a-half-million, **not** 12.5 million

Example: one-third, **not** 1/3

Example: 33-percent, **not** 33%

Example: three-fourths or three-quarters, **not** 3/4

Example: 75-percent or point-7–5, **not** 75% **or** .75

Example: one-16th **not** 1/16

Round Figures

Don't be afraid to round off numbers to make them easier to understand. If it's 1,604, it's perfectly okay to write "about 16-hundred." You can round off numbers in most instances, but sometimes you'll want to be specific. Don't round off numbers when you report deaths or whenever specific figures are more meaningful.

When using rounded-off numbers, you should use words like *more than, nearly, about and slightly less than* to let your listeners know you're not using EXACT figures.

Example: 593 **becomes** nearly 600

Example: 3,489 **becomes** about 35-hundred

Example: 13,323 **becomes** about 13-thousand-300

Example: 687,982 **becomes** almost 700-thousand

Example: 1,000,550 **becomes** a little more than one-million

Example: 999,879 **becomes** slightly less than one-million

Telling Time

We've already seen how time can often be an important element in a story. Write time so the newscaster can read it easily. When you report time, NEVER use *a.m.* or *p.m.* Instead use *this morning, tomorrow evening, tonight, tomorrow afternoon* and similar terms. They're more conversational. In addition, use numerals for hours and minutes notation. Use two zeroes to indicate whole hours.

Example: 5:30 this morning, **not** 5:30 a.m.

Example: 2:45 this afternoon, **not** 2:45 p.m.

Example: 6:15 yesterday evening, **not** 6:15 p.m. yesterday

Example: 8:00 tonight, **not** 8:00 p.m.

When you use *o'clock* in your copy, use numerals to indicate the hour and minutes.

Examples: 1:00 o'clock . . . 2:00 o'clock . . . 5:00 o'clock . . . 9:00 o'clock . . . 10:00 o'clock . . . 11:00 o'clock . . . 12:00 o'clock

Limit your use of "o'clock" to on-the-hour references only. "O'clock" sounds odd when you include minutes.

Examples (poor): 3:15 o'clock . . . 4:30 o'clock . . . 5:45 o'clock . . . 8:10 o'clock

Examples (better): 3:15 this afternoon . . . 4:30 this morning . . . 5:45 this evening . . . 8:10 tonight

When you're dealing with a combination of hours, minutes and seconds, use our basic number rules.

Example: Magee ran the mile in four-minutes-and-13-seconds.

Example: The kissing marathon lasted 72-hours-and-nine-minutes.

Example: Her time was two-hours-10-minutes-and-eight-seconds.

Exceptions to Numbers Rules

As you've probably noticed, there are some exceptions to our rules for numbers. Times of day (hours and minutes), addresses and phone numbers can be written using numerals even if they are less than nine.

Example: 7:30

Example: 1-1-1-6 Daffodil Road

Example: 2-3-2-23-97

Example: 2-3-2-2-3-9-7

In addition, don't start a sentence with a numeral. If you want to begin a sentence with a number, SPELL OUT the number even if it's greater than nine. Don't use numerals at the beginning of a sentence. It looks odd and could be confusing.

Example (poor): 25 people died in the accident.

Example (better): Twenty-five people died in the accident.

One last thing to remember. You SPELL OUT *hundred* only when the number is greater than one-thousand. When the number is less than one-thousand, use numerals.

Example: 1,300 **becomes** one-thousand-300 or 13-hundred

Example: 600 **DOES NOT become** 6-hundred or six-hundred

Numbers Test #1

Look over the following three groups of numbers. Pick out the one that has *all* the numbers written in correct radio-TV news style.

Group A: one, six, 15, six-hundred, 897, 1,500, 1/4, $16, 8-billion

Group B: one, six, 15, 600, 897, 15-hundred, one-fourth, 16-dollars, eight-billion

Group C: one, 6, fifteen, 600, eight-hundred-97, 1,500, one-fourth, sixteen-dollars, 8,000,000,000

If you think group A is correct, turn to page 55.

If you think group B is correct, turn to page 56.

If you think group C is correct, turn to page 57.

Group A? Maybe it wasn't clear that 10 through 999 are written out as arabic numerals.

Six-hundred should be *600*.
1,500 should be *15-hundred*.
1/4 should be *one-fourth*.
$16 should be *16-dollars*.
8-billion should be *eight-billion*.

You'd better go back and reread the section on numbers. It's important to know how to write them correctly. Numbers are hard to read aloud, so you have to write them in a way that makes them somewhat easier.

After you reread the section, turn to page 56.

You said group B, and you're right. All of the numbers are written in correct radio-TV news style. Try the next group of numbers.

Numbers Test #2

Look over the following list of numbers. If a number is written correctly, place an X in the blank. If a number is written incorrectly, correct it. None of the numbers is at the beginning of a sentence.

A. seven _____

B. ten _____

C. 17 _____

D. twenty-eight _____

E. 83 _____

F. one-hundred _____

G. 3-hundred-76 _____

H. 1,246 _____

I. 25-hundred _____

J. six-hundred-thousand _____

K. 3-million _____

L. $14,000 _____

M. 25-cents _____

N. 1/2 _____

O. one-fourth _____

P. June 24 _____

Q. 1st prize _____

R. 1022 22 Avenue _____

S. 50% _____

T. 11:15 p.m. tomorrow night _____

Check your answers on page 58.

Group C? This is the worst of the three options.

6 should be *six.*
Fifteen should be *15.*
Eight-hundred-97 should be *897.*
1,500 should be *15-hundred.*
Sixteen-dollars should be *16-dollars.*
8,000,000,000 should be *eight-billion.*

You'd better go back and reread the section on numbers. It's important to know how to write numbers correctly. They're hard enough to read aloud, so you should try to make them as easy to read as possible.

After rereading the section on numbers, turn to page 56.

Answers to Numbers Test #2

A. seven: *X*

B. ten: *10*

C. 17: *X*

D. twenty-eight: *28*

E. 83: *X*

F. one-hundred: *100*

G. 3-hundred-76: *376*

H. 1,246: *one-thousand-246* or *12-hundred-46*

I. 25-hundred: *X* or *two-thousand-500*

J. six-hundred-thousand: *600-thousand*

K. 3-million: *three-million*

L. $14,000: *14-thousand-dollars*

M. 25-cents: *X*

N. 1/2: *one-half* or *50-percent*

O. one-fourth: *X* or *25-percent* or *one-quarter*

P. June 24: *June 24th*

Q. 1st prize: *first prize*

R. 1022 22 Avenue: *10–22 22nd Avenue*

S. 50%: *50-percent* or *one-half*

T. 11:15 p.m. tomorrow night: *11:15 tomorrow night*

If you missed more than two, go back and reread the entire section on numbers and take the test again. If you missed two or less, you're ready for bigger things.

Go on to the next page.

Approximation Test

You're heading into the home stretch on numbers. All you have to do is round off or approximate the following numbers using proper radio-TV news style.

A. 1,616 _____

B. 9.48 million _____

C. 9,487 _____

D. 49.96% _____

E. 297 yds. _____

F. 1,989 lbs. _____

G. 15.96 oz. (liquid) _____

H. 15.96 oz. (weight) _____

I. 101% increase _____

J. 24¢ _____

K. 5,278 ft. _____

L. 5,751,837 _____

M. $75,193 _____

N. 11.82 in. _____

O. 8.2368 _____

Check your answers on the next page.

Answers to Approximation Test

I used *about* for all the approximations, but any of the appropriate approximation words—*nearly, slightly more than* or *slightly less than*—would be acceptable. The important thing is to be sure to let audience members know that you are approximating.

A. 1,616 **becomes** about 16-hundred *or* about one-thousand-600

B. 9.48 million **becomes** about nine-point-five-million *or* about nine-and-a-half-million *or* about nine-million-500-thousand

C. 9,487 **becomes** about 95-hundred *or* about nine-thousand-500

D. 49.96% **becomes** about 50-percent *or* about one-half

E. 297 yds. **becomes** about 300-yards

F. 1,989 lbs. **becomes** about two-thousand-pounds *or* about a ton

G. 15.96 oz. (liquid) **becomes** about 16-ounces *or* about a pint

H. 15.96 oz. (weight) **becomes** about 16-ounces *or* about a pound

I. 101% increase **becomes** about a 100-percent increase *or* about double *or* about twice as much

J. 24¢ **becomes** about 25-cents *or* about a quarter

K. 5,278 ft. **becomes** about 53-hundred-feet *or* about five-thousand-300-feet *or* about a mile

L. 5,751,837 **becomes** about five-million-750-thousand *or* about five-point-75-million *or* about five-and-three-quarter-million

M. $75,193 **becomes** about 75-thousand-dollars

N. 11.82 in. **becomes** about 12-inches *or* about a foot

O. 8.2368 **becomes** about eight-point-two-five *or* about eight-and-a-quarter

▶ PUNCTUATION

Practical Punctuation

Punctuation has one purpose in radio-TV newswriting—to help the newscaster read the copy more easily and better. Most punctuation in radio-TV newswriting is limited to the period, dash, question mark and comma.

Three periods (. . .) are good to use when you want to indicate a pause. A dash (—) can do the same thing. A dash is often used instead of parentheses in radio-TV newswriting.

Example: According to researchers at Midcity University . . . broccoli could be the next wonder food. Scientists from the National Institute for Clinical Education—better known as NICE—say a daily dose of broccoli might help us all live longer . . . but more tests are needed.

Don't be afraid to "dot" and "dash" up your copy. The more readable it is, the better it is.

▶ COPYEDITING

Correctable Errors

Some wise man once said, "To err is human." If that's true, radio-TV newswriters are among the most human humans in the world. I'm talking about typographical errors now, not factual or content errors.

No matter how good a typist you are, when you get in a hurry or start thinking faster than you type, you're bound to start making mistakes. Computers have made it a lot easier to make corrections, of course, but you might not always have the time to redo a flawed script. In such cases, you'll have to make corrections on the copy that's already been printed.

You may already know the copyediting symbols that are used in newspaper writing. Well, FORGET THEM. Forget them in radio-TV newswriting, anyway.

Seeing something like the following isn't going to help the newscaster much. In fact, it will probably just confuse him.

He failed the exam.

He the failed exam.

The should didn't work.

Example: Do it _this_ way **OR** do _it this_ way **OR** do it _this_ way.

If your copy _starts_ to look _like_ a _giant_ roller _coaster_, you're better off blacking out the entire sentence and writing it over.

Try to keep your copy as clean as possible. Clean copy is easier to read. The following are other examples of acceptable radio-TV news style copyediting.

Example: He will fly to Washington tomorrow.

Example: The Dodgers beat the ~~Pittsburgh~~ Pirates 4-to-1.

Example: Jennifer Warren _of East Midcity_ died in the crash.

The insertion symbol is used only for a word or a group of words. It is NOT used to insert a letter or a group of letters. If you have to add a letter or a couple of letters to a word, black out the incorrect version and print in the correct version.

Example (poor): Winston sc_o_red three first-half touchd_ow_ns.

Example (better): Winston ~~sc[e]ed~~ _scored_ three first-half ~~touch[dfns]~~ _touchdowns._

▶ SCRIPT STYLE

Putting It on Paper

Nearly every radio and television station has a scripting style that's a little different from any other, but for the rest of this learning experience, you'll be using the following guidelines.

1. Type or write on full-size sheets of paper—8.5 × 11.
2. Type or write on one side of the paper only.
3. Double-space copy.
4. Use uppercase and lowercase letters.
5. If you type, use a 60-space (or 60-character) line. A full 60-character line equals :03, so 20 lines of 60 spaces each equals about one minute of copy; 200 words equals about one minute.
6. Use separate sheets of paper for each story.
7. Don't divide words or numbers or hyphenated phrases at the end of a line and continue them on the next line. End each line with a complete word.

8. Slug each story in the upper left-hand corner with a one-word or two-word summary of what the story is about, followed by your name and the date.

Example: Fire deaths
Wulfemeyer
3/10/09

Script Formats

Radio Reader Story

For radio reader stories, use the following format:

Downtown Library
Hunter
4/26/09

Midcity is getting a new, downtown library after all. The

Board of Supervisors approved the 25-million-dollar project this morning.

Last week, the Board voted to delay the project for at

least five years, but Mayor Ronald Moore agreed to some budget

modifications that freed up enough money to fund the new

library. The new 80-thousand-square-foot library will be

built on city-owned land at the corner of Broadway and Market.

Construction is scheduled to start next month.

Radio Actuality Story

For radio actuality stories, use the following format:

Downtown Library
Hunter
4/26/09

Midcity is getting a new, downtown library after all. The Board of Supervisors approved the 25-million-dollar project this morning. Last week, the Board voted to delay the project for at least five years, but Mayor Ronald Moore agreed to some budget modifications that freed up enough money to fund the new library. Moore says he's glad things worked out.

(Moore Cut)

IN: "We really need. . . ."

OUT: ". . . some tough decisions."

TIME: :12

The new 80-thousand-square-foot library will be built on city-owned land at the corner of Broadway and Market. Construction is scheduled to start next month.

Radio Reporter Voicer/Wraparound Story

For radio reporter voicer/wraparound stories, use the following format:

Downtown Library
Hunter
4/26/09

Midcity is getting a new, downtown library after all. K-

TIM's Lynda McFadden is live where the new library will be

built.

———————————————————————————
(McFadden Voicer)

IN: "The new library . . ."

OUT: ". . . I'm Lynda McFadden."

TIME: :40
———————————————————————————

Construction of the new 80-thousand-square library is

scheduled to start next month.

Television Reader Story

For television reader stories, use the following format:

Downtown Library
Hunter
4/26/09

TALENT: Midcity is getting a new, downtown library after all. The

Board of Supervisors approved the 25-million-dollar project

this morning. Last week, the Board voted to delay the

project for at least five years, but Mayor Ronald Moore

agreed to some budget modifications that freed up enough

money to fund the new library. The new 80-thousand-square-

foot library will be built on city-owned land at the corner

of Broadway and Market. Construction is scheduled to start

next month.

Television Picture/Graphics Story

For television stories that feature pictures, maps, charts or graphics, use the following format:

Downtown Library
Hunter
4/26/09

TALENT:	Midcity is getting a new, downtown library after all. The Board of Supervisors approved the 25-million-dollar project this morning.
TAKE MAP:	The new 80-thousand-square-foot library will be built on city-owned land at the corner of Broadway and Market.
TALENT:	Last week, the Board voted to delay the project for at least five years, but Mayor Ronald Moore agreed to some budget modifications that freed up enough money to fund the new library. Construction is scheduled to start next month.

Television Video Story

For television stories that feature video, use the following format:

Downtown Library
Hunter
4/26/09

| TALENT: | Midcity is getting a new, downtown library after all. The Board of Supervisors approved the 25-million-dollar project this morning. |

| TAKE VIDEO/VO: | Last week, the Board voted to delay the project for at least five years, but Mayor Ronald Moore agreed to some budget modifications that freed up enough money to fund the new library. The new 80-thousand-square-foot library will be built on city-owned land at the corner of Broadway and Market. |

| TALENT: | Construction is scheduled to start next month. |

Television VO/SOT Story

For television stories that feature video and a soundbite (VO/SOT), use the following format:

Downtown Library
Hunter
4/26/09

TALENT:	Midcity is getting a new, downtown library after all. The Board of Supervisors approved the 25-million-dollar project this morning.
TAKE VIDEO/VO:	Last week, the Board voted to delay the project for at least five years, but Mayor Ronald Moore agreed to some budget modifications that freed up enough money to fund the new library. Moore says he's glad things worked out.
TAKE SOT FULL:	IN: "We really need. . . ." OUT: ". . . some tough decisions." TIME: :12
TAKE VIDEO/VO:	The new 80-thousand-square-foot library will be built on city-owned land at the corner of Broadway and Market.
TALENT:	Construction is scheduled to start next month.

▶ SUMMARY

Look over the following summary of what we've covered so far in this learning experience. After you've done that, you'll be ready to write some stories.

1. Don't parrot source copy. Use your own words.
2. Write short sentences, but keep a natural conversational flow.
3. Trim excess words.
4. Write tightly, but explain the significance of the story and include all the important details.
5. Use simple words.
6. Don't cram sentences full of separate facts. Take facts one at a time, a sentence at a time.
7. Make your copy easy on the ear *and* easy on the eye.
8. Leads should set the tone of each story. Write them so they could logically follow, "Hey, Jill, guess what I just heard?"
9. Make sure you have all names spelled correctly.
10. Include pronunciation guides for difficult names and words.
11. Place titles before names. Extremely long titles can be broken up or placed after a name.
12. Place ages before names. Use ages only when they're important to the story or when you don't have any other way to identify a person.
13. Place addresses after names and use "who lives at" or "of" to precede street numbers, names or general locations.
14. Attribution always comes before what was said.
15. Don't worry about synonyms for *says* or *said.*
16. Paraphrase direct quotes unless they're colorful.
17. Don't be afraid to repeat words. There's no need to seek synonyms.
18. Use personal pronouns.
19. Use contractions.
20. Use present tense, active voice verbs as often as possible.
21. Beware of abbreviations. SPELL OUT words the way you want them to be read.
22. Place time elements in sentences so they sound natural.
23. Write numbers so they're easy to read.
24. Round off numbers to make them more memorable.
25. Take care with fractions and decimals. Make sure they're understandable.
26. Don't use symbols. SPELL OUT $, ¢, %, &, # and all the rest as words.
27. Use punctuation to help the newscaster read your copy.
28. Keep your copy clean.
29. Limit your use of newspaper copyediting symbols. Black out mistakes completely and print in corrections.
30. Think and write the way you talk.

▶ THE BIG TIME

If you don't feel you're ready to tackle writing a few stories on your own now, go back and glance over the sections you haven't mastered before taking the big plunge. If you feel confident and are ready to go, you can start by looking over the following suggestions for putting radio-TV news stories together.

Remember what you've already learned about leads. They set the tone for your story. They should tell the listener what the story is going to be about.

After the lead, the rest is pretty much up to you. Depending on the type of information you're dealing with, you might want to follow up the lead with some of the specific details of the story. You should try to include all the important details and facts, or at least as many as you can in the allotted time.

Include the causes and reasons for actions, events and statements. The WHY of every story is important. Someplace in your story be sure to include WHY the story is important. WHY it is significant. WHY it is newsworthy. And WHAT it means to the listeners.

Sometimes the WHY comes out of a story naturally. Other times you have to dig it out and point it out to your listeners. For example, if your city council just approved $900,000 for some new playground equipment, you'd want to explain what all the money is going for—specific things—and how much it's going to cost each individual taxpayer, as well as WHY the new equipment is needed.

Think of your story as a series of main points and supporting evidence for each of the main points. Prioritize the main points and then link the supporting evidence with the appropriate main point. The first part of your story should focus on the most important main point and its related supporting evidence. If you have more time to fill, move to the second main point and its supporting evidence. Keep going until you hit the desired length for your story.

A good way to end a story is with some background information. You might mention some of the things that led up to the event you're reporting. If you're talking about a person, you might mention some of his or her other jobs, titles or accomplishments. You might mention some of the lesser details or possible future developments that might be caused by the event, action or statement you're writing about. You also might mention what the next step will be or likely will be.

Don't forget to include the source of your information—the attribution—if the subject matter requires it.

Keep these suggestions in mind as you look over the information on page 72. For the next few writing assignments, pretend you are a newswriter for a radio station in Midcity. Midcity could be in any state.

► **EXERCISES**

Komodo Dragons Story

Write a 20-second story on the Komodo dragons' new home. If you're typing, use a 60-space line. Seven FULL lines should be about 20 seconds. If you're writing out the story in longhand, about 70 words should equal 20 seconds.

MIDCITY ZOO

FOR IMMEDIATE RELEASE
CONTACT: CAROLE TOWNE

PUBLIC AFFAIRS

A moat filled with "dragons" was unveiled for the public at the Midcity Zoo today—but the moat was not the kind associated with medieval castles, and the dragons were not mythological monsters but real live reptiles.

The moat is part of an exhibit just completed that will house the Zoo's two Komodo dragons, the world's largest lizards from the Indonesian island of Komodo and surrounding smaller islands. The reptiles were released into their new home today by Lt. General Victor Krulak, president of the Midcity Zoological Society, and Jerry H. Sanders, Zoo reptile curator.

The new exhibit, adjacent to the Zoo's present Reptile House, was built at a cost of $654,000 and measures sixty by thirty feet. It features enclosed, radiant-heated quarters for the dragons, a pool, extensive landscaping, and a 6-foot-deep moat across which Zoo visitors view the lizards.

The $654,000 was donated to the Zoological Society by the Dorothy Chang Foundation of Midcity.

The dragons had been in their heated indoor quarters for a day to allow them time to become acclimated to that part of their new exhibit. Today was the first time the reptiles were allowed access to the exhibit's outdoor areas.

##########

After you've written your story, turn to the next page to see how one radio-TV newswriter handled it.

Komodo Dragons Story Model

Zoo dragons
Wulf
4/20/08

The Komodo (Koh-MOH-doh) dragons at the Midcity

Zoo have a new home. It's right next to the Reptile House and

it has all the comforts—radiant heat . . . a pool . . . lots of

plants and a six-foot-deep moat to keep out unwanted visitors.

All that luxury cost the zoo 654-thousand-dollars. The

Dorothy Chang Foundation donated the money. Komodo

dragons come from Indonesia and are the world's largest

lizards.

#########

Komodo Dragons Story Analysis

Let's analyze this story. Compare your version as we go through the various elements of the story.

1. The lead sets the tone for the story. It tells what the story is about.
2. After the lead, we get some details: where the exhibit is, what it has, how much it cost, and where the money came from.
3. The story ends with a little background information—what Komodo dragons are and where they come from. This is a good way to get out of a story. It's a natural ending. What more is there to say that's really important?

Endings are sometimes difficult to write. It's hard to decide what information to end with. *Sound* has a lot to do with it. After you've written a few stories, you'll get to where you'll be able to *hear* the ending. You'll put a sentence together and it will just *sound* like the logical place to end the story. When you're reading over the source copy, keep alert for such information. It sometimes makes writing easier if you know what you're going to end with before you start writing.

Did you remember to include a pronunciation guide for Komodo? Did you bother to look it up? Remember, it helps the newscaster if you include how to pronounce unknown or unusual names or words.

Did you use the proper style for writing numbers (*two* dragons, *six*-foot-deep moat, *60-by-30*-feet, *654-thousand*-dollars)?

If you used Victor Krulak, did you put his title in the right place and SPELL OUT *Lieutenant*? Remember, titles come before names.

Did you change the sentence about who donated the money from a passive voice sentence into an active voice sentence?

If you follow all the guidelines in this workbook, your stories will be easy for a newscaster to read and easy for audience members to understand.

Record your story and the model. Play them back and decide which one *sounds* better to you.

Try writing another 20-second story from the information on the next page. You obtained the information after talking with your sources at the Midcity Police Department.

Traffic Deaths Story

(All information obtained from the Midcity Police Department.)

Traffic accident at 7:43 a.m. today.

Only one car involved.

Two men killed.

Names have not been released pending notification of next of kin.

Accident occurred near Northside Recreation Center.

Driver apparently lost control of car after trying to avoid something on Carson Ave.

45-ft. of skid marks were found at scene leading to the spot where car left road.

Car, a late model Toyota, left roadway, traveled up a slight embankment, hit a telephone pole, and flipped over.

"The driver obviously just lost control of the car and couldn't keep it on the road," according to Sgt. Jane Saunders, Midcity Police spokesperson.

The fatalities were number 45 and 46 in Midcity so far this year.

##########

After you've written your story, turn to the model on the next page.

Traffic Deaths Story Model

Traffic Deaths
Kelly
5/3/08

Two men died in a one-car accident this morning near

the Northside Recreation Center. Police say the driver

probably tried to avoid something on the road and lost

control of the car. It skidded 45-feet . . . ran up a slight

hill . . . hit a telephone pole . . . and flipped over. The

names of the men won't be released until their families have

been notified. Midcity's traffic death toll is now 46

for the year.

##########

Traffic Deaths Story Analysis

Let's analyze this story.

1. Right at the start we find out what happened: two men died in a traffic accident. This story could start with a verbless lead, too.

   Example: Two more traffic deaths in Midcity this morning.

   Both the verbless and the emphasis lead could logically follow, "Hey Jack, did you hear?"

2. After the lead, we get some details—how the accident probably happened and the fact that the names haven't been released yet. Did you modify the formal and stilted, "pending notification of next of kin?" People don't talk this way, so don't write this way. Write conversationally.
3. The story ends with a form of background information—the number of people who have died in traffic accidents so far this year. Does it seem like a logical place to end?

Did you use the quote from the police spokesperson? It really doesn't add much does it? You probably do need some attribution for the information about the cause of the accident. The exact cause hasn't been proven yet.
Record your story and the model. How do they *sound*?
Try another 20-second story. It's on the next page.

Cancer Money Story

(Research)

(Washington)—A PROFESSOR AT THE UNIVERSITY OF
IOWA'S SCHOOL OF MEDICINE SAID TODAY THERE SHOULD
BE A 500-MILLION DOLLAR INCREASE FOR CANCER
RESEARCH FOR NEXT YEAR. APPEARING BEFORE THE
SENATE APPROPRIATIONS COMMITTEE IN WASHINGTON,
D.C., DR. ERIC WULF TESTIFIED THE MONEY WOULD
BE USED FOR FINDING AN EFFECTIVE CURE FOR CANCER.
CURRENTLY, THE ADMINISTRATION HAS BUDGETED
900-MILLION DOLLARS FOR NEXT YEAR. WULF IS
ARGUING THAT CONSULTATIONS WITH OTHER CANCER
ORGANIZATIONS AND PROGRAM DIRECTORS HAVE
CONVINCED HIM THAT THE CURRENT BUDGET IS TOO
LOW, THAT ANOTHER 500-MILLION DOLLARS CAN AND
SHOULD BE EFFECTIVELY USED. WULF ADDED THAT THE
500-MILLION DOLLAR INCREASE SHOULD BE ALLOCATED
FOR GRANTS IN THE FIELD OF CANCER RESEARCH.

##########

After you've finished writing your story, turn to the next page and look at the way a professional newswriter handled it.

Cancer Money Story Model

Cancer Money
McFadden
6-10-08

A University of Iowa professor says the federal government
should kick in another 500-million-dollars for cancer
research next year. Doctor Eric Wulf of Iowa's School of
Medicine told a U-S Senate Committee that the
900-million-dollars already budgeted is not enough. He
says the extra money is needed to pay for research
grants so an effective cancer cure can be found.

#########

Cancer Money Story Analysis

Let's analyze this story.

1. The lead tells what the story is about—more federal money is needed for cancer research. (At least Dr. Wulf thinks so.) We find out WHO says more money is needed, HOW MUCH money is needed, and WHEN it's needed.
2. In the second sentence we get some details—WHY the money is needed and TO WHOM Dr. Wulf directed his plea.
3. In the last sentence we find out WHAT the extra money would be used for and another part of WHY it's needed—to find an effective cure for cancer.

How does your story compare? Do you have as much information? Is it clear and easy to understand? Did you use the proper style for all of the numbers? Did you use delayed identification and start the story with Dr. Wulf's title rather than his name? Did you spell out "Doctor?"

Record the source copy, your story and the model. How do they sound? Is yours as easy on the ear? The source copy was supposedly written for radio or television. Do you think it's conversational?

Look over the source copy on the next page. Write a 30-second story from it. That's 10 lines of typed copy, or 100 words.

Sports Arena Story

(BLOOMBERG)

(Midcity)—THE MIDCITY BOARD OF SUPERVISORS LAST
NIGHT DIRECTED CITY CLERK ABBEY OSTREM TO PERFORM
VALIDATION CHECKS OF SIGNATURES ON PETITIONS IN THAT
DRIVE AGAINST DR. LAWRENCE BLOOMBERG'S SPORTS WORLD
DEVELOPMENT. PRIOR TO LAST NIGHT, "CITIZENS CONCERNED
FOR MIDCITY," A LOCAL ACTIVIST GROUP, HAD TURNED IN
3,000 SIGNATURES IN AN ATTEMPT TO PUT THE DEVELOPMENT
TO A PUBLIC VOTE. LAST MONTH, SUPERVISORS GAVE
TENTATIVE APPROVAL FOR THE DEVELOPMENT THAT INCLUDES
SINGLE-FAMILY HOMES, CONDOMINIUMS, AND A SHOPPING
PLAZA. THE DEVELOPMENT WOULD CENTER ON A SPORTS
ARENA FOR BLOOMBERG'S PROFESSIONAL BASKETBALL TEAM,
THE MIDCITY MAVERICKS, OF THE WORLD BASKETBALL
ASSOCIATION. LAST NIGHT CITIZENS CONCERNED FOR
MIDCITY TURNED IN ANOTHER 1,900 SIGNATURES, ACCORDING
TO BOARD SPOKESPERSON ROBERT SCOTT. ONLY 3,500
SIGNATURES ARE NEEDED TO BRING THE ISSUE TO A VOTE.
IF THE CITY CLERK VALIDATES THE APPROPRIATE NUMBER OF
SIGNATURES, THE PUBLIC VOTE WILL BE HELD 6 WEEKS FROM
TOMORROW, SAID SCOTT.

##########

After you've written your story, look over the model on the next page.

Sports Arena Story Model

> Sports Arena
> Robinson
> 7/28/08
>
> The Board of Supervisors wants the city clerk to check the
> validity of the signatures on petitions in that drive to stop
> Doctor Lawrence Bloomberg's Sports World development. The
> Citizens Concerned for Midcity group has been collecting names
> to force a public vote on the issue. The group has collected
> about five-thousand signatures and only 35-hundred are needed.
>
> Bloomberg wants to build a sports arena for his Midcity
> Mavericks at the center of the housing and shopping development.
>
> If enough of the signatures are valid, the vote will be held
> six weeks from tomorrow.
>
> ##########

Sports Arena Story Analysis

Let's analyze this story.

1. Once again the lead tells what the story is going to be about. We get the names of all the participants and the parts they're playing in this little drama.
2. We find out how many signatures have been turned in and how many are needed to bring the issue to a vote.
3. We also get a little background information to finish off the story, just in case some of the listeners haven't been keeping up with what undoubtedly has been a very prominent and ongoing story. In addition, we get some information about what is likely to happen next and when the vote might be taken.

The source copy is a little confusing, and there is at least one major element missing: WHY. Why does the citizens group want to block the project? You'll often come across these gaping holes in source copy. If you can, fill them by making phone calls or checking other sources. If you can't fill them, do the best you can with what you have.

How did your story come out? Did you have trouble getting through the source copy? It is difficult. If you got the number of signatures collected and the number needed (using the proper style), if you mentioned the citizens group in connection with the drive to stop the development, and if you mentioned Dr. Bloomberg, you did a good job.

Did you add up the two figures that dealt with the number of signatures? About 3,000 were turned in originally and another 1,900 were added, which brings the grand total to about 5,000. You owe it to your listeners to do this simple addition. Be on the lookout for ways to simplify numbers. Check their accuracy, too! Make sure they make sense and make sure they're correct.

Record the source copy, your story, and the model. How do they *sound*? The source copy was supposedly written for radio or television. Do you think it's very listenable? How about your story? The model?

Try another 30-second story over the source copy on the next page.

Supervisor Controversy Story

City of Midcity
MEMORANDUM

File No.:   2796
To: News Media
From: Carl Johnson, Assistant to the Mayor
Subject: Mayor Jack Shelley's response to "Weak Supervisor" claim

You have requested Mayor Shelley's response to Supervisor Donna
Loren's testimony to the Charter Revision Committee Tuesday night as
reported in the *Midcity Times*.

The following is the Mayor's statement:

"I think it is nonsense to suggest, as Ms. Donna Loren has done,
that those members of the Board of Supervisors who were appointed are
weaker than those who were elected. Since their appointment, each of
the four supervisors Ms. Loren refers to has run or has vowed to run for
election. So each has had the courage to come before the voters.

"Now neither Ms. Loren nor I have participated in the appointment
of a Board member. But I greatly doubt that appointees are selected on
the basis of being 'least offensive' as Ms. Loren suggests. That certainly
would not be the criterion I would apply, and I'm certain this Board
would look to qualifications and appoint the person it felt most
qualified. Some of the Board's strongest members have been appointed.

"Finally, I would agree with Ms. Loren that if a Board is weak, it is
not because of form or structure. The only real limitation on legislative
power is the legislator's initiative, imagination and persuasiveness."

cc: members of the Board of Supervisors

##########

After you've written your story, check the model on the next page.

Supervisor Controversy Story Model

Supervisor Controversy
Lopez
7-29-08

Mayor Shelley says Supervisor Donna Loren's claim that

the four appointed members of the Board of Supervisors are

weaker than the elected members is a bunch of nonsense. In

fact . . .Shelley says some of the Board's strongest members

have been appointed. He says the four were picked not because

they were the least offensive as Loren suggests, but because they

were the most qualified. And Shelley says since their appointment,

each of the four has run or has promised to run for election.

Loren made her accusations at the Charter Revision Committee

hearing Tuesday night.

#########

Supervisor Controversy Story Analysis

Let's analyze this story.

1. The lead gives the audience members the whole story in a nutshell. The mayor thinks Supervisor Loren is way off base.
2. Next comes the mayor's justification for his statements. (Appointed members are some of the strongest. They were the most qualified. They have run or will run for election.)
3. The writer ties the story off with a little background information. (What started the whole thing—Loren's claims at the Charter Revision hearing.)

In this kind of story, you probably can assume that most audience members know something about Loren's charges, so you can start your story with the mayor's response.

It would be perfectly correct if you started the story with something like "Mayor Shelley has responded to Supervisor Loren's claim that the four appointed members of the Board of Supervisors are weaker than the elected members. Shelley says the charge is a bunch of nonsense."

You also might shorten the first sentence of the lead. "Mayor Shelley has issued a strong response to Supervisor Donna Loren's complaints about some of her fellow supervisors." Shelley says Loren's claim that the appointed members are weaker than the elected members is a bunch of nonsense."

Remember, there are several "correct" ways to write this story or any other story for that matter. The important thing is to get the vital, significant information to your audience members. The model stories and all the other material in this learning experience are designed to help you do just that, and to do it in a way that is easy for a newscaster to read and easy for audience members to understand.

Record your story and the model story. How do they *sound*? Does yours sound as good? Better?

The best way to improve your writing is to write, write, write and write some more. After you have the basics down, you just have to keep writing until it starts to come easy for you.

If you had some problems writing any of the reader stories, or if it took you longer to write the stories than you would have liked, don't worry. After you've written 40 to 50 stories, you'll start to get the hang of it.

Try writing one more 30-second story from the copy below. You're still working in Midcity.

USO Story

> **(CHAPIN/USO)**
>
> (Midcity)—THE MIDCITY USO SAYS IT WANTS THE
> $100,000 ALLEGEDLY PROMISED TO IT BY GARY CHAPIN,
> THE ORGANIZER OF THE "COAST GUARD GIFT PAC" PROGRAM.
> AN ATTORNEY FOR THE USO SAID HE'S WRITTEN TO THE STATE
> ATTORNEY GENERAL TO FORCE CHAPIN TO HAND OVER
> THE MONEY. HE SAID CHAPIN PROMISED TO GIVE THE USO
> A PERCENTAGE OF THE PROCEEDS FROM THE "GIFT PAC"
> PROJECT, IN WHICH CHAPIN SOLICITED DONATIONS HE USED
> TO SEND PRESENTS TO COAST GUARDSMEN. CHAPIN NOW SAYS
> HE CAN'T PAY SINCE A LATER PROGRAM OF HIS CALLED "HELP
> FOR NAVY WIDOWS" IS $100,000 IN DEBT. IN THE "NAVY
> WIDOWS" PROGRAM, CHAPIN PROPOSED TO GIVE SELECTED
> WIDOWS A CAR AND A FREE VACATION. NO DECISION FROM
> THE STATE ATTORNEY GENERAL IS EXPECTED FOR AT LEAST
> 30 DAYS.
>
> ##########

After you've written your story, turn to the next page for a look at the model story.

USO Story Model

USO
Yamashita
12-5-08

The Midcity U-S-O says the organizer of the "Coast Guard Gift Pac" program owes it 100-thousand-dollars. The U-S-O says Gary Chapin (CHAY-pihn) promised it some money from the proceeds. Chapin says he doesn't have the money, because one of his other programs . . . "Help for Navy Widows" . . . is in the red. An attorney for the U-S-O is asking the state attorney general to help clear up the problem. No decision is expected for at least a month, though. In the "Gift Pac" program, Chapin sent presents to Coast Guardsmen. In the "Navy Widows" program, he wanted to give each widow a new car and a free vacation.

#########

USO Story Analysis

Let's analyze this story.

1. The lead tells what the story is going to be about.
2. The facts of the story come next—the name of the organizer, the promises, the programs and their failures, and what the USO plans to do to get its money.
3. At the end, a little background information is provided to help audience members remember who Chapin is.

Did you use "delayed identification" for Gary Chapin? You don't want audience members to miss his name, so give them a chance to get ready for it. I hope you remembered the correct form for writing numbers and you remembered to put hyphens between U-S-O. You're writing for the ear—so your listeners will understand your story easily—but you're also trying to write so the newscaster will be able to read your copy easily.

Record all three of the versions—source, your own and the model. Do they all *sound* the same, or is one better than the others? Why do you think one is better? What is it about the one that *sounds* good to you that is different from the others?

Enter the wonderful world of writing introductions for actualities, soundbites and reporter packages in the next section.

PART 3
Writing Introductions

▶ INTRODUCING RECORDED COMMENTS FROM SOURCES

Actualities and Soundbites

Introductions to radio actualities and television soundbites should set up the recorded comments from sources and help audience members make sense of the comments. Introductions to actualities and soundbites must be part of the "conversation" you're having with your audience members. It is crucial that actualities and soundbites flow naturally and logically from their introductions.

Example: The Board of Supervisors has approved a 25-million-dollar plan to revitalize public parks in Midcity, but some local experts don't like the project. Midcity University Biology Professor Eric Jefferson opposes the plan for two main reasons.

(JEFFERSON CUT)

"The plan is not comprehensive enough. Some communities will benefit, but too many others won't. And for what it will do, it's way too expensive."

Notice how the writer made sure to set up the comment by letting audience members know what the plan is and what it will cost. The recorded comment flows naturally from such an introduction. After the cut plays, the writer will be able to add more details about the plan and what proponents and opponents think about it. Such details could come before the recorded comments, of course.

Here are some additional guidelines for writing introductions to actualities and soundbites:

(1) Name the speaker. Make it clear who is making the recorded comments. You don't want audience members to have to wonder about who's speaking. You want them to concentrate on what is said.

Example: Midcity University Biology Professor Eric Jefferson says the plan has problems.

(JEFFERSON CUT)

"The plan is not comprehensive enough. Some communities will benefit, but too many others won't. And for what it will do, it's way too expensive."

---

(2) Use complete sentences to introduce the speaker's recorded comments. Don't use partial sentences or "dangling" introductions. Technical difficulties might occur and cuts might not play. A complete sentence introduction makes it easier and more professional to deal with such technical difficulties.

Example (poor): Midcity University Biology Professor Eric Jefferson is against the plan because . . .

Example (better): Midcity University Biology Professor Eric Jefferson is against the plan for two main reasons.

Example (better): Midcity University Biology Professor Eric Jefferson is against the plan.

Example (better): Midcity University Biology Professor Eric Jefferson opposes the plan.

Example (better): Midcity University Biology Professor Eric Jefferson doesn't like the plan.

Example (better): Midcity University Biology Professor Eric Jefferson says the plan is flawed.

(3) Don't "echo" the source's recorded comments in the introduction. The introduction should not be the same as the first words of the recorded comments. The introduction should set up the comments, not repeat them.

Example (poor): Midcity University Biology Professor Eric Jefferson says the plan is not comprehensive enough.

(JEFFERSON CUT)

"The plan is not comprehensive enough. Some communities will benefit, but too many others won't. And for what it will do, it's way too expensive."

Example (better): Midcity University Biology Professor Eric Jefferson doesn't like the plan for two main reasons.

Example (better): Midcity University Biology Professor Eric Jefferson says the plan has flaws.

(4) Don't use the "when asked if, here's what he had to say" technique. Using this technique is the lazy way out. You can do better than this. You can be more creative and more conversational.

Example (poor): When asked if he liked the plan, here's what Midcity University Biology Professor Eric Jefferson had to say.

Example (better): Midcity University Biology Professor Eric Jefferson isn't happy with the plan.

Example (better): Midcity University Biology Professor Eric Jefferson says the plan doesn't cover enough and it costs too much.

▶ INTRODUCING REPORTER PACKAGES

Voicers, Wraparounds and Packages

Introductions to reporter voicers, wraparounds and packages serve many of the same purposes as introductions to actualities and soundbites. Introductions must grab the attention of audience members. Introductions must set up the information contained in the reporter's story. Introductions must let audience members know the name of the reporter.

Whenever possible, try to incorporate some interesting aspect of the story in the sentence that includes the name of the reporter.

Example: Lots of excitement at the City Council meeting this afternoon. And reporter Janet Baines was there for all of it.

Example: More than four-thousand classic car fans are in town for the annual convention of the Association of Classic Car Collectors. Reporter Mark Dobbins sat in on the opening session.

Example: Fire destroyed a downtown warehouse this afternoon. Reporter Caitlynn Cabot was on the scene before firefighters arrived.

Example: A new Northside housing project is set to open next week, but reporter Alex Arenas has discovered that the builders violated a number of city housing codes.

A word of caution: Don't go overboard in your efforts to incorporate an aspect of the story in your introduction. Introductions must make sense and flow well, so if you can't come up with a natural-sounding aspect of the story, don't force it. Be careful about using a pun or a "play on words." You might think your introduction is clever and witty, but audience members might find it confusing or inappropriate. They might not understand the reference you're making. They might not "get the joke." In addition, remember that audience members aren't going to see your words, so making clever use of homonyms will not find an appreciative public.

Example: Midcity University started football practice today. We sent reporter Jeff Garcia to tackle the story. (This could work, but why risk it?)

Example: A new bed-and-breakfast inn opens this weekend in the heart of the downtown business district. Reporter Diane Wong went "inn" search of what it has to offer. (So? Remember, your listeners or viewers won't be able to SEE your "clever" use of *inn* for *in.*)

Example: A local turkey rancher is creating quite a stir this holiday season. Reporter Carol Carr gobbled up the story. (Isn't this a bit too cutesy?)

Example: The fish are really biting at area lakes. Reporter Ted Easton baited his hook to get a line on the story. (One pun is bad enough, why go for two?)

Example: A local lumberyard has come up with a new way to use sawdust. Reporter Gary Kim logs in with this story. (Hmm. Do reporters really "log" in?)

Example: The new Astor College of Optometry opens next week. Reporter Alicia McMaster checked out the "sight" of the new campus. (Again, no one will SEE your use of *sight* instead of *site.*)

Example: Central High School's girls' basketball team is ranked number two in the country. Reporter Stephanie Ishida went one-on-one to find out why. (This really doesn't make sense, does it?)

If you can't logically and easily incorporate some aspect of the story in the introduction, simply use one of the traditional voicer, wraparound or package introductions rather than create an inappropriate, goofy, forced or weird sentence.

Example: Janet Baines reports.

Example: Mark Dobbins has the details.

Example: Alicia McKay has the story.

Example: Tom Johnson explains.

Example: Carol Carr has more.

Example: Jeff Garcia has more on the story.

Example: Here's reporter Kent Davis.

Example: Stephanie Ishida is live at the scene.

Example: Tim Chang has this live report.

Example: We go live to reporter Courtney Moore.

Example: Reporter Maria Gonzales is live in the newsroom.

Example: Reporter Juan Fernandez is live in the K-T-I-M satellite center.

Some stations require or encourage writers to include call letters before the reporter's name when introducing a voicer, wraparound or package. You can have the newscaster voice the letters individually or you can use an accepted variation of the call letters.

Example: K-T-I-M's Janet Baines reports.

Example: K-TIM's Mark Dobbins has the details.

Example: K-T-I-M's Alicia McMaster has the story.

Example: K-T-I-M's Tom Johnson explains.

Example: K-TIM's Carol Carr has more.

Example: K-TIM's Jeff Garcia has more on the story.

Example: Here's K-T-I-M reporter Kent Davis.

Example: K-TIM's Stephanie Ishida is live at the scene.

Example: K-T-I-M reporter Tim Chang has this live report.

Example: We go live to K-T-I-M reporter Courtney Moore.

Example: K-TIM reporter Maria Gonzales is live in the newsroom.

Introductions for Actualities and Soundbites

Here's your chance to see how well you can do writing introductions for radio actualities and television soundbites. From the following information, write a :35 actuality story. You'll need 30 seconds of newscaster copy (8+ full lines) to go along with the 10-second actuality. Be sure to introduce the actuality properly.

Firefighters Pay Story

INFORMATION:

(1) According to a state-wide salary survey released at 8:00 a.m. this morning, pay for most Midcity firefighters is generally subpar when compared to pay for 35 other fire departments in the state.

(2) 78% of the departments surveyed pay firefighters more than Midcity pays.

(3) The Midcity Fire Department employs 363 firefighters.

(4) Survey was commissioned by Midcity Mayor Ronald Moore to assist with salary negotiations with the union for Midcity's firefighters, the Midcity Firefighters Association.

(5) Average pay for a Midcity firefighter is $83,000.

(6) Average pay for firefighters statewide is $93,750.

(7) Survey cost $20,000 to conduct.

(8) The Midcity Firefighters Association is demanding a 10% pay increase. Mayor Moore has included a 3% increase in his preliminary budget proposal.

(9) Representatives for the Midcity Firefighters Association have declined to comment on the survey and the mayor's salary proposal, but the union has scheduled a news conference for tomorrow morning at 9 a.m. and they promise to comment then.

(10) Recorded comment from Mayor Ronald Moore: (Time = :10)

"We can't give 10%, but we might be able to afford 5%. We value what the firefighters do, but our budget is very tight."

Turn to the next two pages to see models for the firefighters pay hike actuality story.

Firefighters Pay
Sanders
11/8/08

A survey shows Midcity firefighters earn less than most

other firefighters in the state. The average salary for

Midcity firefighters is 83-thousand-dollars. That's about

11-thousand-dollars below the state average. The Midcity

Firefighters Association wants a 10-percent pay hike, but

Mayor Moore has budgeted just a three-percent raise for the

firefighters.

(MOORE CUT)
IN: "We can't give . . ."
OUT: ". . . is very tight."
TIME: :10

Representatives from the Midcity firefighters' union have

scheduled a news conference for tomorrow morning to

respond to the mayor's salary offer.

#########

Firefighters Pay Story Model 2

Firefighters Pay
Valenzuela
11/8/08

Midcity firefighters are among the lowest paid firefighters in the state. They earn an average salary of 83-thousand-dollars a year. That's more than 11-thousand-dollars less than the state average. The Midcity Firefighters Association wants a 10-percent pay hike, but Mayor Moore has proposed a three-percent increase.

(MOORE CUT)
IN: "We can't give . . ."
OUT: ". . . is very tight."
TIME: :10

Representatives from the Midcity Firefighters union say they'll talk about the Mayor's salary proposal at a news conference tomorrow morning.

#########

Turn to the next page for an analysis of the actuality stories.

Firefighters Pay Story Analysis

The leads for both stories explain what the stories are about—low pay for the Midcity firefighters. Some supporting evidence is provided to back up the main point provided in the leads.

Notice how the writers set up the actuality. They included information about the salary numbers and the pay-hike percentages. By doing so, they help the actuality flow naturally and help audience members understand and make sense of the content of the actuality. The writers named the speaker, used a complete sentence to introduce the actuality and didn't echo the first comments of the source.

How does your version compare to the models?

Actuality Introduction Sentences

Write five different sentences that might be used to introduce the actuality from Mayor Ronald Moore. These sentences would be inserted right before the cut airs and right after adequate information has been provided to set up the actuality.

Example:

A survey shows Midcity firefighters are among the lowest paid firefighters in the state. Local firefighters earn an average salary of 83-thousand-dollars. That's about 11-thousand-dollars less than the state average. The Midcity Firefighters Association wants a 10-percent pay hike, but Mayor Moore has budgeted for a three-percent raise for the firefighters. **(Insert introduction here!)**

(MOORE CUT)

"We can't give 10%, but we might be able to afford 5%. We value what the firefighters do, but our budget is very tight."

Introduction Sentence One: ....

....

Introduction Sentence Two: ....

....

Introduction Sentence Three: ....

....

Introduction Sentence Four: ....

....

Introduction Sentence Five: ....

....

Turn to the next page to see some model sentence introductions.

Actuality Introduction Sentences Models

1. Moore says the firefighters want too much.

2. Moore says he'd like to give the firefighters more, but times are tough.

3. Moore says the M-F-A's salary demands are out of line.

4. Moore says he might be able to up the offer some, but the city can't afford to meet the M-F-A's salary demands.

5. Moore says the M-F-A's salary demands are unrealistic.

6. Moore says there just isn't enough money in the budget to offer much more.

Actuality Introduction Sentences Analysis

Notice how different the introduction sentences are, yet they all say essentially the same thing. The M-F-A wants more money, but the city can't afford to pay any more. All of the introductions do a good job setting up the content of the actuality.

How did your introduction sentences compare to the models? If you came up with sentences that help the actuality flow naturally and logically, you did a good job. If you named the speaker, you did a good job. If you avoided the "echo effect," you did a good job. If you used a complete sentence, you did a good job.

Try your hand at writing another :40 actuality story from the information on the next page. Use the proper script format for this one.

Salmonella Outbreak Story

From the following information, write a :40 actuality story. You'll need 30 seconds of newscaster copy (10 full lines) to go with the 10-second actuality.

INFORMATION:

(1) Scientists for the U.S. government say they have pinpointed the source of the latest outbreak of salmonella in the U.S.

(2) Nearly 400 people in 43 states have fallen ill in the last three months from salmonella poisoning. No deaths reported, though.

(3) Midcity has recorded 4 cases of salmonella poisoning in the past three months.

(4) Contaminated peanut butter is suspected as the source of the salmonella outbreak.

(5) Investigators say they have strong evidence that suggests Farmer Bill's peanut butter is the culprit. Farmer Bill's is the 4th largest brand of peanut butter in the U.S. behind Jif, Peter Pan and Skippy.

(6) According to the Center for Disease Control and Prevention, consumers are encouraged to discard jars of Farmer Bill's peanut butter with a product code of "1818" on the lid. The number denotes the plant where the peanut butter was manufactured.

(7) Based on the results of preliminary tests, investigators suspect the contaminated peanut butter was produced at the Sylvester, Georgia plant of Foodco Inc., the parent company of the Farmer Bill's line of food products. The code number for the Georgia plant is 1818. The plant was shut down yesterday.

(8) Salmonella sickens about 40,000 people in the U.S. each year. About 600 people die from the disease in the U.S. each year.

(9) Salmonella poisoning can cause diarrhea, fever, dehydration, abdominal pain and vomiting.

(10) More tests at the Foodco plant will be conducted next week.

(11) An estimated 975,000,000 pounds of peanut butter are sold in the U.S. each year.

(12) Recorded comment from Dr. Sandra Sanchez, an epidemiologist at the Center for Disease Control and Prevention: (Time = :10)

"We're not exactly sure how the dangerous germ got into the peanut butter, but it's likely the contamination came from dirty jars or processing equipment."

Turn to the next page to see a model for the salmonella actuality story.

Salmonella Outbreak Story Model

Salmonella Outbreak
Cassidy
6/14/08

Government scientists think they've finally found the source of the salmonella outbreak that's sweeping the country. Almost 400 people have reported experiencing the symptoms of salmonella poisoning in the last three months, including four cases in Midcity.

Scientists are blaming the outbreak on tainted jars of Farmer Bill's peanut butter. But an epidemiologist at the Center for Disease Control and Prevention, Doctor Sandra Sanchez, says more research needs to be done.

(SANCHEZ CUT)
In: "We're not exactly . . ."
Out: ". . . or processing equipment."
Time: :10

If you have jars of Farmer Bill's peanut butter with the product code of 18–18 on the lid, you should throw them away.

Turn to the next page for an analysis of the model story.

Salmonella Outbreak Story Analysis

The lead explains what the story is about and includes the latest development in this ongoing story. The extent of the problem is mentioned and the local impact is included. Next, the writer pinpoints the expected source of the problem. In setting up the actuality, the writer provides the speaker's title and name. In addition, the writer provides needed information to set up the recorded comments. After the cut, the writer gives information about how consumers can identify the tainted peanut butter and what they should do if they have a jar of it.

Did you use proper style for numbers?

400 people
code number 18–18
40-thousand-people
fourth largest brand
43 states
600 people
975-million-pounds

How did your story compare to the model? Did you set up the recorded comments well? You named the speaker before the cut, right?

Let's try writing some introductions for reporter packages. Turn to the next page.

▶ INTRODUCTIONS FOR PRE-RECORDED STORIES FROM REPORTERS

Here's your chance to test your skill at writing introductions for reporter voicers, wraparounds and packages.

Traffic Deaths Story

From the following information, write FIVE different reporter introductions.

INFORMATION:

(1) 26 vehicles crashed on a foggy Interstate 15 north of town last night.
(2) 37 people injured.
(3) 10 people died.
(4) Property damage estimate: $500,000
(5) This is the deadliest single traffic accident in state history.
(6) The previous state record for deaths in a single traffic accident was nine.
(7) The first vehicles involved in the crash collided about 11:10 p.m.
(8) Vehicles continued to pile into each other for about 10 minutes before highway patrol officers could close off the highway.
(9) KTIM's Teri Conner was heading home after her shift and was one of the first people stopped by the highway patrol near the crash site. She was the first reporter at the scene. She reports on the incident.

Introduction One: . . . .
. . . .

Introduction Two: . . . .
. . . .

Introduction Three: . . . .
. . . .

Introduction Four: . . . .
. . . .

Introduction Five: . . . .
. . . .

Turn to the next page to see some examples of reporter introductions for the massive traffic accident story.

Traffic Deaths Story Reporter Introduction Models

1. Ten people died in a massive traffic accident on Interstate 15 last night. K-TIM's Teri Conner just missed being involved in the pileup.

2. A record-setting traffic accident on Interstate 15 last night. And K-T-I-M reporter Teri Conner was almost one of the victims.

3. Multiple deaths and injuries in a massive traffic accident on foggy Interstate 15 last night. Teri Conner was the first reporter at the scene.

4. Ten people died and 37 others were injured in a traffic accident involving more than two dozen vehicles last night on Interstate 15. Our Teri Conner was heading home on the freeway at the time and arrived at the crash scene just moments after the last of the collisions.

5. A record number of deaths last night in a massive traffic accident on foggy Interstate 15. K-T-I-M reporter Teri Conner was on the freeway at the time of the accident and just missed being part of the death and destruction.

6. A record number of deaths in a huge traffic accident on a foggy local freeway last night. Reporter Teri Conner was just a few minutes away from being involved in the crash.

Turn to the next page for an analysis of the reporter introductions.

Traffic Deaths Story Reporter Introduction Analysis

You almost have to use at least a couple of numbers to introduce reporter Teri Conner's story. With deaths, injuries, property damage and a numbered freeway, you'd have to be very creative to avoid mentioning at least one number. Try to keep your use of specific numbers to a minimum, though, especially in an introduction to a reporter voicer, wrap-around or package. It's better to let reporters include the specific figures and statistics. They can use several sentences to help audience members understand the significance of the amounts, sizes and so on.

Example 6 avoids numbers, but it lacks impact compared to the others. Examples 2, 3 and 5 at least try to keep the numbers to a minimum. Example 4 just fires away with four number-related references in the first sentence. That's probably too many, but the introduction seems to work fairly well.

Note how the coincidence of Teri Conner being on the freeway at the time of the accident is worked into each introduction. All the examples are much better ways to mention her name than the traditional "Teri Conner reports," "Teri Conner explains," and so forth.

How did your introductions compare to the model examples? Record your examples and the models. Which ones sound the best to you?

Turn to the next page and try your hand at writing five more introductions for a pre-recorded reporter package.

Killer Whale Story

From the following information, write FIVE different introductions for the killer whale story.

INFORMATION:

(1) Trainer at Oceanland in Midcity was bitten by a killer whale and taken to the bottom of the tank during a show at 3 pm this afternoon.
(2) KCTI has acquired video of the attack from a spectator who was using a home video camera.
(3) 3,000 people were in the audience and witnessed the attack.
(4) The trainer, Riley Loren, 29, suffered puncture wounds to her leg, but is recovering in a local hospital, according to an Oceanland spokesperson.
(5) Kiko, the female orca that bit the trainer, has been performing at Oceanland for 9 years.
(6) A male orca bit another trainer 8 months ago during a training session, but the wounds were not serious.
(7) KCTI reporter Carlos del Toro begins his report standing in front of the water tank at the killer whale show venue.

Introduction One: ....

....

Introduction Two: ....

....

Introduction Three: ....

....

Introduction Four: ....

....

Introduction Five: ....

....

Turn to the next page to see some examples of reporter introductions for the killer whale story.

Killer Whale Story Reporter Introduction Models

1. A killer whale attacked a trainer during a show at Midcity's Oceanland this afternoon. Carlos del Toro reports from the park.

2. A trainer at Midcity's Oceanland is recovering this evening after a killer whale attacked her during a show this afternoon. KCTI reporter Carlos del Toro has the details.

3. A killer whale bit a trainer and dragged her under the water during a show at Midcity's Oceanland this afternoon. KCTI reporter Carlos del Toro has more on the attack.

4. More than the usual excitement at Midcity's Oceanland this afternoon. A killer whale attacked a trainer during a show. Reporter Carlos del Toro has the story and video of the attack.

5. Another killer whale attack at Midcity's Oceanland. Today's attack has put a trainer in the hospital. Our Carlos del Toro has video of how it happened.

6. A trainer at Midcity's Oceanland is lucky to be alive this evening. A killer whale attacked her during a show this afternoon. KCTI's Carlos del Toro reports on what three-thousand people witnessed.

Turn to the next page for an analysis of the reporter introductions.

Killer Whale Story Reporter Introduction Analysis

Introductions 1, 3 and 5 all feature the attack by the killer whale. Introductions 2 and 6 focus a bit more on the trainer. Introduction 4 is a bit vague, but it would likely arouse some interest.

Introductions 1, 2, 3 and 6 all use complete sentences. Introductions 4 and 5 begin with verbless leads, but they work fairly well.

Take a look at the different words used to indicate a report by Carlos del Toro is about to air:

Reports from the park
Has the details
Has more on the attack
Has the story and video of the attack
Has video of how it happened
Reports on what three-thousand people witnessed

No two are exactly alike. This shows how it's possible to vary the introductions to packages so that even if a package airs several times, at least the introduction can be fresh.

How do your introductions compare to the models? Do you have as much variety? Do you have some verbless leads?

Turn to the next page to test your skill at writing reporter introductions for breaking news stories and live reports.

Introductions for Live Reports

Warehouse Fire Story

From the following information, write FIVE different reporter introductions for the live, breaking news report from the scene of a furniture warehouse fire by KTIM's Kent Davis.

INFORMATION:

(1) A fire at the Tucker Furniture warehouse started about 90 minutes ago.
(2) The 50,000 square foot warehouse is fully engulfed in flames.
(3) Value of building estimated at $2.5 million.
(4) Value of contents of building estimated at $3.75 million.
(5) Firefighters are battling the blaze, but officials don't think they'll be able to save the building or any of its contents.
(6) No word on how the fire might have started.
(7) The warehouse is located at 1583 N. Mollison Dr.
(8) The 10:00 p.m. newscast will begin with the live report.
(9) Kent Davis has been on the scene for about 75 minutes. He'll do his report standing about 100 yards away from the warehouse, but the sights and sounds will be clear in the background.

Introduction One: ....
....

Introduction Two: ....
....

Introduction Three: ....
....

Introduction Four: ....
....

Introduction Five: ....
....

Turn to the next page to see some examples of reporter introductions for the live report about the furniture warehouse fire.

Warehouse Fire Story Reporter Introduction Models

1. We have breaking news this evening. The Tucker Furniture warehouse on North Mollison Drive is burning out of control. K-TIM's Kent Davis is live at the scene.

2. The Tucker Furniture warehouse on North Mollison Drive is on fire at this hour. Let's go live to K-T-I-M's Kent Davis.

3. A fire at the Tucker Furniture warehouse on North Mollison Drive has been raging for about 90 minutes. Our Kent Davis is as close to the action as a reporter can be.

4. Fire is destroying the Tucker Furniture warehouse on North Mollison Drive at this hour. Reporter Kent Davis has been on the scene for more than an hour. We go to him now, live.

5. A fire is raging at the Tucker Furniture warehouse on North Mollison Drive. K-TIM's Kent Davis is standing by live.

6. A multi-million-dollar fire at the Tucker Furniture warehouse on North Mollison Drive. K-T-I-M's Kent Davis has a live report.

   Turn to the next page for an analysis of the reporter introductions.

Warehouse Fire Story Reporter Introduction Analysis

Note how five of the six model introductions use present-tense verbs. This helps drive home the immediacy aspect of live reports. In addition, we get the basic information in each of the introductions—fire, type of warehouse, location, name of reporter.

There aren't too many variations associated with letting audience members know that a live report is coming up. Look at example 3. What do you think of it? It says nothing about a "live" report, but the implication is clear. Try to vary your use of "has a live report," "we go to her live," "is standing by live," and so on. Make sure audience members know they're going to hear/see a live report, but avoid using the exact same wording for every live story.

How did your introductions compare to the model examples? Record your examples and the models. Which ones sound the best to you? Which ones convey the best sense of immediacy?

Turn to the next page for another opportunity to write reporter introductions for a live news report.

Squirrel Jet Story

Write FIVE different introductions for KTIM's Lori Kelly's live report from the scene of an emergency landing by a Midwest Airlines jet.

INFORMATION:

(1) A Midwest Airlines jet was forced to make an emergency landing at Midcity International Airport this morning about 10 a.m.

(2) Jet had just taken off when pilot radioed the control tower and reported hearing strange noises in the cockpit.

(3) Upon landing, investigators found a squirrel in one of the overhead bins in the cockpit.

(4) Flight 2717 was scheduled to fly to Los Angeles. The Boeing Co. 777 had 196 passengers and 7 crew members.

(5) According to an airline spokesperson, it would be possible for a squirrel to chew through wires on a plane and that could cause serious problems.

(6) KTIM reporter Lori Kelly will report live from the airport. She'll begin her report inside the cockpit of the plane.

Introduction One: ....

....

Introduction Two: ....

....

Introduction Three: ....

....

Introduction Four: ....

....

Introduction Five: ....

....

Turn to the next page to see some examples of introductions for Lori Kelly's live reports.

Squirrel Jet Story Reporter Introduction Models

1. A squirrely situation out at the Midcity Airport this morning. Lori Kelly has a live report.

2. A Midwest Airlines jet made an emergency landing this morning at the Midcity Airport. Lori Kelly is standing by live.

3. Strange noises in the cockpit forced a Midwest Airlines jet to make an emergency landing at the Midcity Airport this morning. Lori Kelly is live in the cockpit of the troubled plane.

4. A Midwest Airlines jet on its way to Los Angeles had to make an emergency landing at the Midcity Airport this morning. Lori Kelly explains what happened in this live report.

5. Things got a little squirrely in the cockpit of a Midwest Airlines jet this morning. K-Tim's Lori Kelly is live with more on this nutty story.

6. A squirrel gave more than 200 people aboard a Midwest Airlines jet a bit of a scare this morning. Lori Kelly reports live from the cockpit of the plane.

Turn to the next page for an analysis of the reporter introductions for the "squirrel in the cockpit" story.

Squirrel Jet Story Reporter Introductions Analysis

Introduction 1 features a verbless lead and a play on words. The "squirrely situation" is a bit of a stretch, but it works somewhat. Using "squirrely" might be too cutesy for some audience members. Take care and KNOW YOUR AUDIENCE!

Introduction 2 is a bit generic. It's really better to include some unique, story-specific information to help interest audience members. Emergency landings happen relatively often, so what's unique about this one? Always look for and think about emphasizing the unique aspects associated with an event or issue. That's what NEWS is all about.

Introduction 3 does a better job of highlighting what's different about this particular emergency landing. It's still a bit vague, but it will likely grab interest.

Introduction 4 features another generic "emergency landing" lead. At least some additional information is provided (jet was on its way to Los Angeles), but more specificity would help.

Introduction 5 features the "squirrely" reference again. This one at least pinpoints the action (in the cockpit). What do you think of the reference to "this nutty story?" Too much?

Introduction 6 doesn't give away the punchline, so it will likely attract interest. The "bit of a scare" reference is a bit of a cliché, but it works in this case.

Notice the ways the reporter is introduced in each model:

Has a live report
Is standing by live
Is live in the cockpit of the troubled plane
Explains what happened in this live report
Is live with more on this nutty story
Reports live from the cockpit of the plane

Do you have as much variety in your introductions? How do your introductions compare to the models? Remember, it's important to tell stories in your own words. In addition, you need to come up with fresh approaches when you're dealing with previously aired material. Sometimes there is not always a better way to write something, but there always is a different way to write something. Just be sure your different way of writing something tells a good story, is accurate, is easy to understand and will interest audience members.

Before we end this learning experience, let's enter the exciting world of writing for graphics and video. Turn to the next page.

PART 4
Adding Visuals

▶ **WRITING FOR TELEVISION**

Turn on the TV

By making it this far, you're well on your way to mastering the basic techniques of radio-TV newswriting. With a bit more practice, you should be able to write simple "reader" stories for both radio and television newscasts. A "reader" story is one that is read by the newscaster without any additional audio or video enhancement, no soundbites from sources, no pictures, no maps, no charts and no video.

Before we finish this self-instructional learning experience, I want to give you an opportunity to try your hand at writing some slightly more complex stories. Writing copy to go with pictures, graphics and video involves all of the concerns we've addressed so far, plus you have to be careful to match the words with whatever viewers are seeing on the TV screen.

There are three basic ways that copy can be written for video, pictures and other visuals.

1. The story is written first, then the visuals are selected, edited and placed to match the words.
2. The visuals are selected and edited first, then the words are written to match the visuals.
3. The words and visuals are considered simultaneously, with appropriate compromises being made to achieve the most effective and frequent matching of words and visuals.

If you can master writing to match pre-selected and pre-edited visuals, you'll easily be able to master the other two methods. The key to matching words and visuals is to look at the visuals or a description of the visuals and determine what information is most closely associated with what visuals.

You don't want to be overly descriptive about what viewers are seeing, but you do want to explain what they're seeing and avoid blatant conflicts between what they're seeing and what they're hearing.

Example (poor): Picture of Martin Boyd   Linda Smith will take over next month.

Example (better): Picture of Martin Boyd   Martin Boyd will step down next month.

When writing to match video, look at the order of the separate scenes to get a sense of how the story will have to flow. Make written or mental notes about what places, actions and people come before what other places, actions and people. Begin formulating your story so that you can be sure to match the major participants in the video as well as major shifts in subject matter or geographic location.

Example:

	SHOT LIST:
1. Fire trucks and flames	:06
2. Fire Captain (Garver)	:03
3. Burning house	:03
4. Homeowner (McFeely)	:06
5. Dog (Sparky)	:06
TOTAL TIME:	:24

Using the example shot list, you'd first have to write some general information about the fire. Then, in order, you'd have to mention the Fire Captain, the house, the homeowner and the significance of the dog.

Once you have the order figured out, you have to concern yourself with matching the words with the visuals. Using the example, you'd need six seconds of information about the fire, the location and the firefighting effort. Next, you'd need three seconds of information about the Fire Captain, three seconds about the house, six seconds about the home-owner, and six seconds about Sparky, the dog. Remember, a FULL line of 60 spaces equals three seconds.

Example:

TAKE VIDEO/VO   The fire started at about 6:00 o'clock and it took

firefighters almost two hours to bring it under

control.

Fire Captain Brenda Garver estimated about

125-thousand-dollars damage was done to the house.

John McFeely says his dog Sparky's barking

woke him up in time to get his family out of the

burning house.

McFeely says Sparky's reward is going to be a new

dog house and steak dinners for a week.

Don't forget that pauses can be used to help you improve your matching of words and pictures. A picture really can be worth a thousand words, especially if the picture has natural sound with it.

Keep pauses to a minimum, though. They should not be overused and are best when video is dramatic and natural sound helps viewers understand what's going on.

Pauses can be inserted in your script in the following ways:

Example: ....(Pause :03)..

Example: ....

Example: ....(Pause until plane takes off)..........................

Be sure to place parentheses around words you don't want the newscaster to read.

As you write your story, be sure to check the timing. If you fall behind the visuals, eliminate some words or even whole sentences. If you get ahead of the visuals, add some words or put in some pauses.

Split Screen

The script format for television writing is somewhat different from radio writing. In many television stations, copy is centered in the middle of the page so that newscasters will be able to read it easily when it's projected onto the lens of the camera via a teleprompter system. Viewers don't see the words, of course, but newscasters do and it helps them maintain eye contact with viewers.

In this learning experience, we'll use a modified style for our television scripts. We'll still use 60-space lines, but we'll shift the copy that we want the newscaster to read to the right two-thirds of the paper. Down the left one-third of the paper, we'll include directions to the technicians who help us get the newscast on the air. Write the directions in ALL CAPS!

Example:

TALENT:	An earthquake rocked Egypt this morning. No deaths or injuries reported, but lots of damage—at least 250-million-dollars worth.
TAKE MAP/VO FULL SCREEN	The center of the quake was about a mile north of Cairo, but people felt the earth move 100 miles away.
TALENT:	The earthquake measured four-point-nine on the Richter Scale.

Use lines to separate the on-camera, reader copy and the copy to be read while a picture or video is being seen by the viewers. Indicate the type of visual to be shown and let the technicians know that the newscaster will continue to read copy while the visual is shown. The VO stands for "voice-over." That means the newscaster's voice will continue to be heard over the visual.

Example:

TALENT:	An earthquake rocked Egypt this morning.
TAKE VIDEO/VO	No deaths or injuries reported, but lots of damage— at least 250-million-dollars worth. The center of the quake was about a mile north of Cairo, but people felt the earth move 100 miles away.
TALENT:	The earthquake measured four-point-nine on the Richter Scale.

In the example scripts, TALENT is used to indicate when you want the newscaster to be seen on camera reading copy. When you want a director to show a picture, map, or chart or to roll video, insert a line and instruct him or her to TAKE MAP, TAKE PICTURE, TAKE CHART or TAKE VIDEO. The VO stands for voice-over and means that the newscaster continues to read even though viewers don't see him or her. FULL SCREEN is included when you want the picture, map or chart to fill the entire television screen rather than be used as an insert over the newscaster's shoulder. Be sure to insert lines between changes in what viewers are supposed to see. Every time you move from TALENT to something else and vice versa, insert a line. It'll help avoid embarrassing moments for newscasters, directors and you.

▶ EXERCISES

Westlake High School Story

Now it's time to write some copy to match a pre-selected map. Take a look at the source copy and the description of the map. Write a 15-second story. That's about five FULL lines of copy or about 50 words. Remember, we're still using 60-space lines. Each FULL line equals three seconds. Be sure to indicate where the map should be inserted. Follow the script format used for the earthquake story on the previous page.

FULL SCREEN MAP:

Highway 95 runs north and south. Madison Avenue runs east and west. Site for the high school is indicated by a big, red square.

SOURCE COPY:

(1) Site for the construction of the new Westlake High School has been selected by the Midcity Board of Education.
(2) 75-acre parcel.
(3) Location is near the intersection of Highway 95 and Madison Ave.
(4) Site selected because of proximity to Highway 95 and service via bus line.
(5) Cost: $85,000,000.
(6) Cost covers land, construction, furniture and other facilities and equipment.

After you've written your story, look at the model story on the next page.

Westlake High School Story Model

Westlake HS
Martinez
6/3/08

TALENT:	The Midcity Board of Education has decided where the new Westlake High School will be built.
TAKE MAP	The Board picked a 75-acre Madison Avenue location,
FULL SCREEN	because it's near Highway 95 and it's on the bus line.
TALENT:	The new Westlake High School will cost about 85-million-dollars.

#########

Westlake High School Story Analysis

Let's analyze this story.

1. The lead gets right to the news: The Board of Education has picked the site for the new high school.
2. The second sentence deals with the precise location of the site. Since that's what the map shows, it is inserted so viewers can hear and see just where the school will be built.
3. After a mention of why the site was selected, we return to the newscaster for information about how much the new school will cost taxpayers.

Did you remember the proper style for *85-million-dollars* and *75-acre* site? Did you spell out *Avenue*? Record your version and the model. Which one sounds better? Why?

Try writing another story that uses a full-screen graphic. Turn to the next page.

SAT Scores Story

Write a 30-second story from the following information. Be sure to insert the chart when you write about the specific test scores.

FULL SCREEN CHART:

	SAT Scores	
	Last Year	This Year
Midcity	1,510	1,530
Nation	1,520	1,520

INFORMATION:

(1) Last year's nationwide average on Scholastic Aptitude Test (SAT) = 1,520.
(2) Last year's Midcity average on SAT = 1,510.
(3) This year's nationwide average on SAT = 1,520.
(4) This year's Midcity average on SAT = 1,530.
(5) First time in a decade that average Midcity SAT scores are higher than national average.
(6) Total possible on SAT = 2,400. Covers critical reading, math and writing skills/knowledge. Each section scored 200–800.
(7) 2nd straight year Midcity SAT scores have increased.
(8) Quote from Midcity School District spokesperson Courtney Lynn:

"Our teachers made a commitment three years ago to help students improve their SAT scores and it looks as if the effort is really paying off. We feel the scores will continue to increase more next year and for many years to come."

(9) Test is taken by high school seniors.
(10) One program given credit for the improved SAT scores is the required fifteen minutes of "free reading" time every day at local high schools, according to Lynn. The program has been in operation for four years.

After you've written your story, check out the model story on the next page.

SAT Scores Story Model

Test scores
Buckalew
6/10/08

TALENT:	More proof that Midcity schools are doing something right. For the second straight year, the Scholastic Aptitude Test scores of local high school seniors are up.
TAKE SCORES CHART FULL SCREEN	The average this year was 15-hundred-30 out of a possible 24-hundred. Last year the average was 15-hundred-10. The increase pushed the local scores above the national average for the first time in 10 years.
TALENT:	School district officials say Midcity teachers have worked hard to help students improve their test scores. Officials expect the scores to increase even more next year.

##########

An analysis of this story is on the next page.

SAT Scores Story Analysis

Let's analyze this story.

1. The lead is a conclusion. Based on the increasing test scores, the writer concludes that local schools must be doing something right.
2. The second sentence is more like a traditional lead. The phrase at the beginning of the sentence could be moved to the end, but at least we get some information about SAT scores, who takes the test, and the upward trend.
3. After stating the general direction of the scores, the writer gets more specific. The chart is inserted as the newscaster talks about the exact numbers and the move past the national average.
4. Finally, after the chart is removed and the newscaster is seen again, the writer explains why the scores have increased and includes the prediction that scores will be even better next year.

Did you write all the numbers in correct radio-TV news style? (*second, 15-hundred-10 OR one-thousdand-510, 15-hundred-20 OR one-thousand-520, 15-hundred-30 OR one-thousand-530, 24-hundred OR two-thousand-400, 10*) Did you use the information about the "free reading" period? It might be worth including.

How does your version compare to the model? Record them both and play them back. Which is more conversational? Remember that we still want the copy to flow in a natural, conversational manner even though we have visual images to worry about.

Try writing another story using a full screen picture. Turn to the next page.

Golden Dollar Story

Write a :30 story from the following information. Be sure to insert the picture when you write about what the coin looks like.

FULL SCREEN PICTURE:

Side-by-side front and back views of the coin. Former President Jimmy Carter's picture is on one side and the Statue of Liberty is on the other side.

INFORMATION:

(1) A new series of $1 coins was released into circulation this morning.
(2) Former US President Jimmy Carter's likeness is on one side of the coin and the Statue of Liberty is on the other side of the coin.
(3) The coins are gold-colored and slightly larger than a quarter.
(4) The Federal Reserve has placed orders for 300 million of the Carter coins from the US Mint.
(5) The new coins are part of a decade-long series honoring former presidents of the United States.
(6) Dollar coins cost $.22 each to make, but last for up to 30 years. Dollar bills cost about $.06 to make, but last less than 2 years.
(7) The US Mint plans to eliminate the $1 bill over the next 5 years.
(8) The legislation that authorized the presidential coins requires that all vending machines have the capability to accept and dispense the new coins.

After you've written your story, check out the model story on the next page.

Golden Dollar Story Model

Golden Dollar
Schneider
4/26/08

TALENT:	A new, golden one-dollar coin starts circulating today.
TAKE DOLLAR PIC:	A likeness of former President Jimmy Carter is on one side of the coin and the Statue of Liberty is on the other side. The U-S Mint is phasing out the one-dollar bill and replacing it with the gold-colored dollar coins.
TALENT:	The new coin is part of the long-running series featuring former U-S presidents. The Federal Reserve has ordered 300-million of the golden Carter coins. The coins cost more to make, but they last about 15 times longer than dollar bills. All vending machines should be able to accept and dispense the new coins.

#########

An analysis of this story is on the next page.

Golden Dollar Story Analysis

The lead gets right to the point—a new, golden, one-dollar coin is on the market. Then the writer includes the information about what's on the coin when viewers are actually seeing the picture of both sides of the coin.

After the picture is taken away, the writer includes some background information—the series, why the coins are being produced, the cost of producing the coins and the fact that vending machines will accept the new coins.

How did your version turn out? Did you insert the picture when the newscaster was talking about what's on both sides of the coin? It's the most logical and appropriate information to match up with the picture. Did you include the exact cost to make the coins compared to the exact cost to make dollar bills? This story has a lot of numbers in it. Sometimes audience members can become overwhelmed when lots of numbers are thrown at them in a story. Look for ways to reduce the number of numbers you have to use in stories. Often, you can combine numbers by doing simple additions, subtractions, multiplications and divisions. Be sure to check your math, though.

Let's complicate things even more. Try writing a 30-second "voice-over" story from the information on the next page. A voice-over is a story that is read by a newscaster while video is seen by the viewers. Remember to look at the shot list to get an idea of the order of the scenes. Organize the information to match the video as closely as possible.

Include some on-camera newscaster copy before and after the 18 seconds of video. The newscaster copy that comes before the video is called an *intro* (short for introduction) and the newscaster copy that comes after the video is called a *tag* or *tail*. Using a 60-character line, you should have about six lines of video copy and about four lines of on-camera newscaster copy.

Measles Shots Story

SHOT LIST:

1.	Long shot of people standing in line at the health center	:06
2.	Medium shot of two mothers holding their children	:03
3.	Medium shot of college student getting a shot	:06
4.	Close-up shot of college student's reaction to shot	:03

TOTAL TIME: :18

INFORMATION:

(1) At 8 a.m. this morning, Eastside Medical Center began giving free measles immunizations. Session ended at 12 p.m.

(2) Free measles shots will be given again next Monday, 8 a.m. to 12 p.m.

(3) Midcity University requires that freshmen provide proof of measles immunization before they are permitted to register for classes.

(4) Most of the shots given to persons younger than 12 years old, but about 33% went to college-age students.

(5) 5,023 immunizations given.

(6) Quote from Dr. Melissa Janell, director of the Eastside Medical Center:

"We've pretty much got measles under control, but we still have to be sure everyone has been immunized. We feel it's important that we do our part to help keep Midcity a healthy place to live and work."

(7) Eastside Medical Center used its own money to provide the shots.

(8) There were five reported cases of measles in Midcity last year, according to Midcity Department of Public Health.

As usual, the model story is on the next page.

Measles Shots Story Model

Measles shots
Kim
7/9/08

| TALENT: | About five-thousand Midcitians got a shot in the arm this morning. |

| TAKE VIDEO/VO | They took advantage of free measles immunizations at the Eastside Medical Center. Most of the shots went to kids, of course, but some college students showed up, too. Midcity University requires that incoming freshmen be immunized against measles before they can sign up for classes. |

| TALENT: | If you missed out on the measles shots today, the Eastside Medical Center will be giving free measles immunizations again next Monday morning starting at 8:00 o'clock. |

##########

An analysis of this story is on the next page.

Measles Shots Story Analysis

Let's analyze this story.

1. The writer takes a few liberties with the lead, but it's interesting and will likely grab interest. The lead is a bit vague, but perhaps the viewers will want to find out just what "shot in the arm" means.
2. The first video scene of people in line runs six seconds, so the writer decided to include information about the location and the type of shots received. She needed two lines to fill the time and came pretty close.
3. The next scene of two mothers and their children runs just three seconds. The writer decided to mention the point that most of the people who received shots were children. Good matching!
4. The third scene of a college student receiving a shot runs six seconds. Here the writer mentions the twist on a fairly routine story. Even though most people think of children when the subject of measles shots comes up, college students need to be immunized, too. Again, good matching!
5. The fourth scene is just three seconds long. Since it is a continuation of the college student getting a shot, the writer continues with information related to why students need shots.
6. After the video ends, the writer has the newscaster give information about the next round of free shots. Sounds like a good ending, don't you think?

Overall, the matching of audio and video is pretty good. How did you do? Did yours match as well? You needed two lines of copy (or copy plus pauses) for the first scene, one line for the second scene, two lines for the third scene, and one line for the fourth scene.

Did you look at the shot list to get an idea of how you had to order the information? Did you recognize that you had to start with some general information about the location, the type of shots and/or the number of people who received shots and then mention kids before giving the information about college students?

Did you use correct style for writing times? It's 8:00 o'clock and 12:00 o'clock NOT eight o'clock or twelve o'clock. Of course, you didn't use a.m. or p.m., right?

Did you use correct style for writing numbers? It's five-thousand or five-thousand-23. Did you approximate the number? The exact number is probably not important in this story.

Record your version and the model. How do they sound? Matching video while still maintaining a logical, conversational flow in your copy is a real art. Don't feel too bad if you had trouble with this story. With more practice, you'll improve.

Try another voice-over story. The shot list and information are on the next page. The entire story should run 45 seconds (15 seconds of on-camera newscaster copy and 30 seconds of copy to go with the video). Be sure to include some on-camera newscaster copy before and after the video. You should have about 10 lines of video copy and about five lines of on-camera newscaster copy.

Delayed Debate Story

SHOT LIST:

1. Wide shot of almost empty auditorium	:06
2. Close-up of clock (7:55)	:03
3. Medium shot of one bored person/empty seats	:03
4. Medium shot of Sanchez and Duncan	:03
5. Wide shot of sparse audience	:03
6. Close-up of Sanchez	:06
7. Close-up of Duncan	:06
TOTAL TIME:	:30

INFORMATION:

(1) Scheduled debate between Board of Supervisors candidates Maria Sanchez and David Duncan did not start on time tonight.

(2) Candidates will debate again tomorrow night at 7:00 p.m. at the Southside Recreation Center. Both vowed to be on time for that one.

(3) Both candidates had attended dinner meetings and were late getting to McFadden Elementary School. Spokespersons for candidates said scheduling conflicts were the real culprits. The candidates simply are trying to attend too many functions and when one event runs long, it affects all the others.

(4) Debate was supposed to start at 7:00 p.m., but candidates did not show up until 7:55!

(5) Pretty good crowd on hand at 7:00—about 150—but by the time the candidates arrived, only about 15 people were still there.

(6) Candidates are running in District Four.

(7) After some discussion, Sanchez and Duncan decided to go ahead with the debate.

(8) Usual issues debated.

(9) One new issue did come up, though. Sanchez said we had to do something to stimulate construction in Midcity. She suggested eliminating the fees charged in connection with building permits. Duncan didn't like that idea. He said such a move would cost the city way too much money. He said he'd consider cutting the fees in half, but that would be as far as he'd go.

After you've written your story, go to the next page for a look at the model story.

Delayed Debate Story Model

Delayed Debate
Washington
10/10/08

| TALENT: | Some scheduling problems for two supervisor candidates this evening and they ended up playing to an almost empty house at McFadden Elementary School. |

TAKE VIDEO/VO   A debate between the two District Four candidates

was supposed to start at 7:00 o'clock, but neither

one showed up until almost 8:00. By that time, most of the

people who had wanted to hear the candidates were gone.

Both Maria Sanchez and David Duncan were delayed

at dinner meetings. When the debate finally started,

Sanchez said she favors waiving building permit fees

to encourage more construction activity in Midcity.

Duncan countered that completely waiving fees

is too drastic. He suggested cutting the fees in half.

TALENT: Sanchez and Duncan promise to be on time for their

debate tomorrow night at 7:00 at the Southside Recreation

Center.

#########

An analysis of this story is on the next page.

Delayed Debate Story Analysis

Let's analyze the candidate debate story.

1. The lead tells what happened. A couple of supervisor candidates had some problems and were late to a scheduled debate. Their tardiness cost them most of their audience.
2. The first scene of video is of the empty auditorium and runs :06. The writer mentions what was supposed to happen and when.
3. The second scene of the clock runs :03 and is matched well with copy about the hour delay.
4. The third scene of a bored, diehard political groupie and a bunch of empty seats runs :03, so the writer mentions the absent throngs.
5. The fourth scene of the tardy candidates runs :03, so logically the candidates should be mentioned here. They are.
6. The fifth scene is what's known as a "cutaway." It's a general scene that is used as a transition between two main scenes. Usually you don't have to match cutaways, so the writer simply continues with details of why the candidates were late.
7. The sixth scene of Maria Sanchez runs :06. Whenever a major participant appears in video, he or she should be mentioned. She is.
8. The seventh scene of David Duncan runs :06. The writer does a good job of matching Duncan with information about what he said.
9. Once we come back to the on-camera newscaster, the writer concludes with information about the next debate. Seems like a logical ending, doesn't it?

How does your version compare with the model? Did you match as often and as well? Did you have the information in the right order? You had to write about the empty room first (:06), then the time problem (:03), the sparse crowd (:03), the arrival of the candidates (:03 + :03), comments from Sanchez (:06), and comments from Duncan (:06).

Did you write all the times in correct style (7:00, 8:00, 7:00 o'clock)? Did your story flow in a conversational manner?

Record your version and the model. How do they sound? Do they sound as if you're *telling* a story rather than *reading* a story?

Try a rewrite of your story if you don't feel you matched well and/or the conversational flow was not all that it could have been.

Try a final voice-over story. The shot list and information are on the next page. The entire story should run 45 seconds (15 seconds of on-camera newscaster copy and 30 seconds of copy to go with the video). Be sure to include some on-camera newscaster copy before and after the video. You should have about 10 lines of video copy and about five lines of on-camera newscaster copy.

Parking Lot Fire Story

SHOT LIST:

1. Wide shot of parking lot	:09
2. Medium shot of Ventura	:06
3. Medium shot of Ford Explorer	:06
4. Wide shot of firefighters/insurance investigators	:09
TOTAL TIME:	:30

INFORMATION:

(1) Fire destroyed eight cars and damaged five others at a Midcity University parking lot this morning. No deaths or injuries, though.

(2) Damage estimate: $250,000. Estimate provided by Susan Ventura, Midcity Fire Department battalion chief. She was in charge of the firefighting efforts.

(3) Fire started about 9:05 a.m.

(4) "We're pretty sure the fire started under the hood of a Ford Explorer," said Ventura. "It's likely that gasoline vapors were ignited by a hot manifold."

(5) The fire occurred in a lot reserved for university employees—staff, faculty and administrators.

(6) Flames quickly spread to adjacent vehicles.

(7) When firefighters arrived, they found several cars burning and at least a dozen more vehicles were in jeopardy, Ventura added. "We were lucky that more cars weren't torched," she said.

(8) Insurance investigators surveyed the damage for at least two hours after the flames were extinguished. They interviewed staffers and talked with firefighters.

(9) Firefighters stayed on the scene until about 1:00 p.m.

(10) After the damaged cars were removed, the parking lot was reopened at 1:00 p.m.

After you've written your story, go to the next page for a look at the model story.

Parking Lot Fire Story Model

Parking Lot Fire
Wulfe
10/10/08

TALENT:	Fire raced through a parking lot at Midcity University this morning. No one was injured, but 13 vehicles were either destroyed or damaged.
TAKE VIDEO/VO	The fire started a little after 9:00 in a faculty-staff parking lot. Eight cars were destroyed and five were damaged, but firefighters say things could have been a lot worse.
Midcity Fire Department Battalion Chief Susan Ventura estimates damage at about 250-thousand-dollars. She says the fire probably started when heat from the engine of a Ford Explorer ignited some gasoline vapors.
When the fire was under control and mop-up activities were underway, insurance investigators took over, interviewing firefighters and the owners of the cars.
TALENT:	It took firefighters and investigators nearly four hours to get things pretty much back to normal and the parking lot reopened about 1:00.

##########

An analysis of this story is on the next page.

Parking Lot Fire Story Analysis

Let's analyze the parking lot fire story.

1. The lead tells what happened. A fire destroyed and damaged cars in a parking lot at Midcity University. It runs about :08.
2. The first scene of video is a wide shot of the faculty-staff parking lot. It runs :09. The writer uses the scene to mention the location and to list the extent of the damage. The possibility of greater damage is included, too. Notice that there are about three lines of copy for the scene. Good matching.
3. The second scene of video is a medium shot of Susan Ventura, a fire department battalion chief. It runs :06. The writer uses this scene to include comments from Ventura related to the amount of the damage and to begin her speculation about how the fire might have started. The two lines of copy match well with the video.
4. The third scene of video is a medium shot of the Ford Explorer. It runs :06. The writer uses this scene to continue Ventura's comments about how the fire probably started under the hood of the Ford Explorer. Again, audience members are hearing about a Ford Explorer when they are seeing a Ford Explorer. Good matching.
5. The fourth scene of video is a wide shot of the parking lot as firefighters and insurance investigators do their jobs. It runs :09. The writer uses the scene to mention the mop-up efforts of firefighters and the work of insurance investigators. The three lines of copy fit nicely and match well.
6. The on-camera tail wraps up the story by giving some information about how long it took to get things back to normal. It's not a bad idea to end with the current status of things. Audience members will likely feel satisfied that they've been given all the information they need to know about the fire when they hear that the parking lot has been reopened.

How does your version compare with the model? Did you match the copy with every scene? Did you have the information in the right order? You had to write about the parking lot first (:09), then mention Susan Ventura (:06), the Ford Explorer (:06), and the mop-up work of the firefighters and the insurance investigators (:09).

Did you write all the times in correct style (9:00, 1:00)? Did you write the numbers in proper radio-TV style? (250-thousand-dollars, eight cars, five cars, 13 vehicles). Did your story flow in a conversational manner?

Record your version and the model. How do they sound? Do they sound as if you're *telling* a story rather than *reading* a story?

Rewrite your story if you don't feel you matched well and/or the conversational flow was not as smooth as you'd like.

If you're ready to move on, try writing a VO/SOT from the information on the next page.

Tree Clean-Up Story

Write a :40 story from the information below. You should have about seven lines of copy for the anchor to read with video and a bit more than three lines of on-camera copy.

INFORMATION:

(1) 162 trees blown over during a wind storm in Midcity yesterday. Most of the fallen trees blocked roadways and driveways. Many fell on cars and trucks parked on the street and in driveways.

(2) City crews worked all last night and are continuing to work today to remove the trees.

(3) Winds yesterday measured as high as 50 mph.

(4) Of the 162 trees that were toppled, 154 were city-owned and 8 were on private property.

(5) City crews respond to mishaps on city-owned land or when city-owned property causes mishaps and when a city right of way is jeopardized, according to Niko Valens, director of the Midcity Streets Division.

(6) Damage estimated at $5,000,000 by Valens. Estimate covers cost of trees, cost of clean-up efforts, and damage caused to cars and trucks when trees fell on them.

(7) Clean-up efforts will continue for the next 24 hours or so, but the clean-up operation is expected to be complete by noon tomorrow, according to Valens.

(8) Valens soundbite: (:09) "It was an amazingly intense storm. I'm actually surprised and we're extremely lucky that we didn't lose more trees and suffer a lot more damage."

SHOT LIST:

1. Wide shot of crews working on fallen trees	:06
2. Medium shot of tree lying across a car	:03
3. Medium shot of a worker using a chainsaw	:06
4. Valens soundbite	:09
5. Wide shot of clean-up activities	:06
TOTAL TIME:	:30

After you've written your story, go to the next page to look at the model story.

Tree Clean-Up Story Model

TALENT:	City work crews continue cleaning-up after yesterday's big wind storm.
TAKE VIDEO/VO/SOT:	The winds, which were clocked as high as 50 miles an hour, blew over 162 trees.
	The trees clogged streets and slammed into cars and trucks.
	Local officials estimate the damage at five-million dollars.
	The Director of the Midcity Streets Division, Niko Valens, says things could have been worse.
SOT FULL	IN: "It was an . . ." OUT: ". . . lot more damage." TIME: :09
TAKE VIDEO/VO/SOT:	Valens says crews will work all day today and throughout the night cutting up the fallen trees and clearing roadways.
TALENT:	Valens says crews worked all last night as well, so he expects the clean-up will be completed by noon tomorrow.

#########

An analysis of this story is on the next page.

Tree Clean-Up Story Analysis

1. The writer begins by letting viewers know that city crews are still working to clean up the mess caused by the wind storm.
2. The first scene of video is a wide shot of clean-up action. It runs :06. The writer uses the scene to mention the speed of the winds and the number of fallen trees.
3. The second scene of video is a medium shot of a tree that fell on a car. It runs :03. The writer uses the scene to mention that in addition to clogging streets, trees fell on top of cars and trucks. Good matching here.
4. The third scene of video is another medium shot of a worker using a chainsaw to cut up a tree. It runs :06. The writer uses the scene to give the damage estimate and to set up the soundbite from Niko Valens, the director of the Midcity Streets Division.
5. The fourth scene of video is the soundbite from Niko Valens. The writer separates the soundbite from the voice-over copy and provides the incue, outcue and time for the soundbite.
6. The fifth scene of video is another wide shot of clean-up activities. It runs :06. The writer uses the scene to mention that crews will continue their clean-up efforts today and tonight.
7. The writer ends the story with the newscaster back on-camera for a "tag" talking about the projected end of the clean-up efforts. This is a good way to end a story—giving a bit of future-related information.

How does your story compare to the model? Does your copy flow in a conversational manner? This story does not require a great deal of specific matching of audio and video, but did you mention damaged cars and trucks when the scene of the damaged car began? Did you insert the soundbite properly? Did you have :15 of video-related copy for the newscaster to read prior to the soundbite? Did you have another :06 of video-related copy for the newscaster to read after the soundbite? Did you include :10 of on-camera copy for the newscaster to read (Intro + Tag)?

Did you write the numbers in proper style?

162 trees
50 miles an hour
five-million-dollars

Record your version and the model for the tree clean-up story. How do they sound? If yours sounds a bit choppy, try a rewrite. If you're satisfied with your story, move on to the next VO/SOT story. This one has a few more specific matching points that you'll need to hit. Turn to the next page.

Car Auction Story

Write a :50 story from the following information. You'll need about 10 lines of copy for the anchor to read over video and about three lines of on-camera copy.

INFORMATION:

(1) Annual Midcity Car Collector's Auction conducted last night.
(2) 152 cars sold.
(3) Most cars sold for $5,000–$250,000.
(4) A 1966 Shelby Cobra sold for $6,500,000.
(5) Kona Hunter, 27, of Midcity, bought the Shelby Cobra.
(6) The price for the Shelby Cobra is the highest price ever paid for an American-made car.
(7) Hunter plans to loan the Shelby Cobra to the Midcity Museum of Popular Culture for one year.
(8) The Shelby Cobra was created/designed by Carroll Shelby. He used a British sports car chassis and a Ford engine. Only 50 Shelby Cobras were manufactured and only 6 still exist.
(9) The Shelby Cobra has all of its original equipment and just 14,000 miles.
(10) Jim Holtzman, 59, of San Diego, CA, sold the Shelby Cobra. Holtzman, the original owner, rarely drove the car and kept it in a garage. He plans to use the money from the sale to pay for a documentary film he plans to make dealing with classic car collecting and restoration.
(11) Hunter soundbite: (:09)

"I love this car and I'd like to keep it all to myself, but I'm going to let the museum have it for a year so everybody will get a chance to see it."

SHOT LIST:

1. Wide shot of new owner inside car revving the engine. Old owner outside car looking on.	:07
2. Medium shot of old owner.	:07
3. Close up of engine.	:05
4. Medium shot of new owner.	:06
5. Hunter SOT FULL	:09
6. Wide shot of cars and auction activities	:06
TOTAL TIME:	:40

After you've written your story, go to the next page for a look at the model story.

Car Auction Story Model

TALENT:	A Midcity man paid the highest price ever for an American car last night at the annual Midcity Car Collectors' Auction.
TAKE VIDEO/VO/SOT:	Twenty-seven-year-old Kona Hunter paid 6-point-5-million-dollars for a 19–66 Shelby Cobra. It's one of only six still in existence. The car's previous owner, Jim Holtzman of San Diego, says he's going to use the money to finance a documentary film about car collecting. Holtzman rarely drove the car, so it has all of its original equipment and just 14-thousand miles. Hunter won't be driving the car right away. He plans to loan it to the Midcity Museum of Popular Culture.
SOT FULL:	IN: "I love this car . . ." OUT: ". . . chance to see it." TIME: :09
TAKE VIDEO/VO/SOT:	More than 150 vintage and classic cars were sold at the auction. Prices ranged from five-thousand-dollars to 250-thousand-dollars.
TALENT:	Carroll Shelby used a Ford engine and a British sports car chassis to create his Shelby Cobra.

##########

Turn to the next page for an analysis of the car auction story.

Car Auction Story Analysis

1. The on-camera lead emphasizes the main news—a man paid a record-setting price for an American car. It runs about :06.
2. The first scene of video is a wide shot of the car with both the new owner and the old owner visible. It runs :07. The writer uses the scene to mention the new owner, the car and the price paid for the classic Shelby Cobra. Good information and good matching.
3. The second scene of video is a medium shot of the former owner. It runs :07. The writer mentions the former owner and what he plans to do with the $6.5 million. Good matching.
4. The third scene of the video is a close-up of the car's engine. It runs :05. The writer mentions the car's equipment and its low miles. Good matching.
5. The fourth scene of video is a medium shot of the new owner. It runs :06. The writer mentions Mr. Hunter again and uses the scene to set up the content of the soundbite. The soundbite flows well from the intro. Another good matching.
6. The writer next indicates the SOT FULL nature of the soundbite and gives the incue, outcue and time of the soundbite.
7. After the soundbite airs, the writer uses the final :06 wide shot of the auction action to mention the number of cars sold and the price range. Good matching, again.
8. The anchor tag runs about :04. It provides some background information about the man who created the Shelby Cobra. A logical ending.

How does your story compare to the model? Did your copy flow in a conversational manner? Did you insert the soundbite properly? Did you have the information in the right order for the video?

1. Car with both new and old owners
2. Old owner
3. New owner
4. Soundbite
5. Auction action

Did you write the numbers in proper style?

Twenty-seven-year-old OR 27-year-old
6-point-5-million-dollars OR six-point-five-million-dollars
five-thousand-dollars
250-thousand-dollars
152 cars OR about 150 cars

Record your story and the model. How do they sound? If your version sounds a bit choppy and/or your matching was off a bit, try a rewrite. The more you write, the better writer you'll become.

Don't forget all the things we've worked on during this learning experience to help the poor old newscaster make some sense of your prose. You might even be the person who has to read your copy, and you have to write well so you can broadcast/cablecast/webcast well.

If you or another newscaster has trouble reading your copy, you can be sure your audience members are going to have even more trouble understanding it. Make your copy easy on the eye as well as easy on the ear.

I know you could go on writing radio-TV news stories for hours, but that's enough for now. However, before you put the workbook away, take one last look at a summary of the material we've covered in this radio-TV newswriting learning experience.

► SUMMARY

1. Write it your way—in your own words. Don't parrot source copy.
2. Write the way you talk.
3. Be brief, but include all the important information.
4. Use simple, easy-to-understand words.
5. Don't stuff your sentences full of separate facts.
6. Your lead should set the tone for the story. It's like a headline, but don't use "headlinese." Be conversational.
7. Include pronunciation guides for unusual names and words.
8. Place titles before names.
9. Write the way you talk.
10. Place attribution before what was said.
11. Place ages before names.
12. Use contractions and personal pronouns.
13. Use present tense verbs whenever you can.
14. Use active voice verbs instead of passive voice verbs.
15. Don't abbreviate. Write out all words as you want them read.
16. Write the way you talk.
17. Write numbers so they're easy to read and understand.
18. Put hyphens between numbers/letters you want pronounced separately.
19. Use punctuation to help the newscaster read your copy easily.
20. Keep your copy clean.
21. Limit your use of copyediting symbols.
22. For introductions to actualities and soundbites, set up the recorded comments well, plus name the speaker, use complete sentences and don't "echo" the recorded comments.
23. Use elements of the story to introduce reporter voicers, wraparounds and packages.
24. Match words with pictures, graphics and video.
25. Write the way you talk.

► CONGRATULATIONS

Give yourself a pat on the back for successfully completing this self-instructional learning experience. You've worked hard and done well.

Keep practicing, though. Schedule time to write at least one story every day. Take newspaper stories and try to write them in radio-TV news style. Visit the web sites of newspapers and rewrite stories you find there.

Listen to radio newscasts and watch television newscasts as often as you can. Analyze and think critically about the way stories are written. Take notes on the stories and try to write your own versions. Visit the web sites of radio and television stations. Many stations archive scripts, plus include audio, video and graphics. Rewrite the scripts and incorporate audio and/or video to practice and develop your skills.

Check out http://news.yahoo.com/business and click on the Press Releases button at the top. You'll find plenty of news releases to rewrite. Visit the web sites of businesses, corporations, colleges, universities and organizations. Hunt for the public relations news releases on such sites. Rewrite the releases as news stories.

Attend events that you know will receive radio-TV news coverage. Take notes and write stories based on the events. Compare your stories to the ones that air on local stations.

Work for campus radio and television stations. See if you can intern or volunteer at local stations. Public broadcasting stations almost always are looking for bright, energetic people to volunteer their time.

There's really no substitute for practicing the craft of radio-TV newswriting. Just do it!

Appendix

VOWELS

A   AY for long A as in *mate*
A for short A as in *cat*
AI for nasal A as in *air*
AH for short A as in *father*
AW for broad A as in *talk*

E   EE for long E as in *meet*
EH for short E as in *get*
UH for hollow E as in *the*
AY for French long E with
accent as in *Pathé*
IH for E as in *pretty*
EW for EW as in *few*
E for middle E as in *per*

O   OH for long O as in *note* or *though*
AW for broad O as in *fought*
AH for short O as in *hot*
OO for O as in *fool* or *through*
U for O as in *foot*
OW for O as in *how* or *plough*

U   EW for long U as in *mule*
OO for long U as in *rule*
U for middle U as in *put*
UH for short U as in *shut*

I   EYE for long I as in *time*
EE for French long I as in *machine*
IH for short I as in *pity*

CONSONANTS

K for hard C as in *cat*
S for soft C as in *cease*
SH for soft CH as in *machine*
CH for hard CH or TCH as in *catch*
Z for hard S as in *disease*
S for soft S as in *sun*
G for hard G as in *gang*
J for soft G as in *general*